2.50

Scout Proficiency Badges

Copyright © 1993
The Scout Association
Baden-Powell House, Queen's Gate, London SW7 5JS
ISBN 0 85165 266 2
Revised Edition
Second Printing November 1997

Introduction

As well as the Scout, Pathfinder, Explorer and Chief Scout's Awards, which you will work for as you progress through Scouts, there are also many Proficiency badges which give you the chance to develop a more detailed knowledge of a particular subject. You will find the requirements for these badges in this book - have a look through and you will soon see that there is a badge for almost every subject that could possibly interest you.

You may have the opportunity to work for some of these badges during Troop Meetings and camps, or perhaps at a special course arranged by your District, but others you will have to work for by yourself. When you feel sure that you are ready to take the badge tell your Patrol Leader or Scout Leader and they will either arrange for you to be examined or give you the name and telephone number of the badge examiner so that you can arrange an appointment for yourself.

The Proficiency badges are divided into five different categories.

Interest badges are intended basically for younger Scouts, although a Scout of any age may gain one.

Pursuit badges are intended mostly for older Scouts but there is nothing to stop you gaining one whilst you are younger as long as you are able to complete all the requirements satisfactorily.

Collective Achievement badges are designed for a group of Scouts, perhaps a Patrol or perhaps just a group of friends, to work for together.

Service badges cover subjects such as first aid and fire fighting which enable you to be of service to other people. It is particularly important that you achieve a high standard to gain one of these badges as other Scouts and members of the public will expect you to know what to do, particularly in emergencies.

Instructor badges. These special badges are available to any Scout who has the knowledge and experience to train other Scouts to Proficiency badge standard. Instructor badges are available for all Proficiency badges except those for which coaching training is not available or those which must be supervised by adults for safety reasons. Full requirements are on page 98.

Badge colours

Interest and Pursuit badges are usually green. Service badges are red and Collective Achievement badges have a green background with a red border. Instructor badges, the fifth category, are the same colour and design as the ordinary badges in the subject but have a gold border. The diagram in the back of your *Scout Record Book* will show you where these badges should be worn.

The Airmanship and Seamanship badges have four progressive stages, the first two of which come in the Interest category and the second two in the Pursuit category. If you are an Air Scout or a Sea Scout you will almost certainly want to work your way through the appropriate badges, but they are available for all Scouts to gain. Each of the Airmanship badges and each of the Seamanship badges is of the same basic design but with a different colour for each of the stages.

Whichever badges you decide to work for, aim for a high standard so that you can be really proud to wear the badges you have gained and, above all, enjoy working for them!

When you need further information, help or advice on the topics covered in this book there should be help locally. Find out if your District or County has got a District or County adviser in that subject. The advisers are there to help you. There is also a fact sheet on each badge available from the Resource Centre at Gilwell Park.

The Programme and Training Department at Gilwell Park will also help you if you need any information or advice on any of the Proficiency Badges. Just write to:

> Scout Section Office, Gilwell Park,
> Chingford, London E4 7QW.
> Fax: 0181 498 5329.
> e-mail: ukgilscout@aol.com.

Note to Patrol Leaders and Scout Leaders

All Scouts should be encouraged to work for Proficiency badges using the requirements as stated. However for some Scouts with special needs certain requirements may need modification in consultation with the Scout, the Patrol Leaders' Council and possibly the Assistant District Commissioner (Special Needs), parents and others, to ensure that all Scouts have an opportunity to work for all badges.

Administrator

Service

1. *Either:*

   Write, with a good legible hand, 250 words prose.

   Or:

   Type 100 words, with not more than five mistakes and show how to clean the machine and replace the ribbon.

   Or:

   Type 200 words on a computer or word processor ensuring that there are no mistakes. Print it out and show how to replace the ribbon or cartridge on the printer.
2. Show an understanding of committee procedure including preparing an agenda and taking minutes.
3. Show a general knowledge of the administrative arrangements of a Scout Group.
4. Know how a personal bank account operates and how to write a cheque.
5. Write a letter on a subject chosen by the examiner.
6. Draft a wording for an invitation card addressed to members of the public in connection with a Group, Troop or Patrol event.
7. *Either:*

   Prepare a press release on a Group event.

   Or:

   Write an article for a Scout magazine reporting a Troop, Group or Patrol event.

   Or:

   Prepare a report to show awareness of the need for safety precautions.
8. Carry out the duties of Secretary of your Patrol, the Patrol Leaders' Council or some other committee not necessarily concerned with Scouting, for a period of three months.
9. Give a short talk to the Troop demonstrating your knowledge of one or two of the above.

Aeronautics

Pursuit

To gain the badge you must complete all the requirements in one of the following alternatives:

A 1. Know the rules relating to access to airfields as laid down in *Policy, Organisation and Rules.*

2. Understand the purpose and operation of ailerons, rudder, elevator and trim on a glider and have the effects of these controls demonstrated in flight.

3. Understand the functions and workings of the altimeter, airspeed indicator and variometer.

4. Assist a glider pilot with the ground handling, hangar parking and launching of his aircraft.

5. Demonstrate the signals used by the glider pilot and forward signaller for the launching of a glider and the procedure for stopping a launch.

B 1. Know the rules relating to access to airfields as laid down in *Policy, Organisation and Rules.*

2. Assist a pilot with ground handling, the picketing of a light aircraft and the preparation of a light aircraft for flight.

3. Understand the purpose and operation of ailerons, rudder, elevator, flaps and trim on a light aircraft and have the effects of these controls demonstrated in flight.

4. Understand the functions and workings of the altimeter, airspeed indicator and engine instrumentation.

5. Demonstrate the marshalling signals used when marshalling powered aircraft. Identify the common signals displayed on the airfield signal square.

6. Understand the R/T procedure for a circuit of an airfield.

C 1. Know the rules relating to access to airfields as laid down in *Policy, Organisation and Rules.*

2. Demonstrate the marshalling signals used when marshalling powered aircraft **or** demonstrate the signals used by a glider pilot and forward signaller for the launching of a glider and the procedure for stopping a launch.

3. Identify the parts of an aircraft and explain their functions in controlling the aircraft.

4. Assist with the ground handling and picketing of a light aircraft or the ground handling, rigging and de-rigging of a glider.

5. Demonstrate the ground checks that have to be carried out before flying a light aircraft or glider.

6. Demonstrate an ability to carry out two of the following:

   (a) Tie knots and make splices used in glider launching equipment.

   (b) Repair a small tear in the fabric surface of a light aircraft or glider.

   (c) Replenish a light aircraft's fuel system

(d) Carry out a pre-use inspection of a parachute and demonstrate how to put it on and take it off.

(e) Assist with the launching of a hot air balloon.

(f) Know the procedure for starting up a piston-engined aircraft.

D 1. Know the rules relating to access to airfields as laid down in *Policy, Organisation and Rules.*

2. Pass or have passed the Paraglider badge.

3. Identify the parts of a round and wing canopy parachute and understand the operation and effects of their control.

4. Understand the airflow through and round a wing canopy parachute and the need for launching into wind.

5. Understand the functions of the launch marshall and demonstrate the signals used.

6. Understand the need for canopy stability on tow and list five common causes of rotation.

Note:

Requirement A also covers motor or power gliders.

Airmanship

JUNIOR AIRMAN
Interest
(green background)

1. Know the rules relating to access to airfields as laid down in *Policy, Organisation and Rules.*
2. From the list of training activities, successfully complete seven items from at least four of the sections.

AIRMAN
Interest
(red background)

1. Hold the Junior Airman badge **or** be at least 11½ years old and complete requirement 1 of the Junior Airman badge.
2. Identify the parts of an aircraft and explain the principles of flight.
3. From the list of training activities successfully complete a further eleven items from at least five of the sections.

LEADING AIRMAN
Pursuit
(grey background)

1. Hold the Airman badge **or** be at least 13 years old and complete requirements 1 and 2 of the Airman badge.
2. Identify the basic clouds and explain how they are formed. Explain how wind speed is measured and how weather can affect various air activities.
3. From the list of training activities successfully complete a further seven items from at least four sections.

MASTER AIRMAN
Pursuit
(gold background)

1. Hold the Leading Airman badge **or** be at least 14 years old and complete requirements 1 and 2 of the Leading Airman badge.
2. Take part in an air experience flight and point out on an air map the features that are overflown. (This can be undertaken in powered aircraft, glider or balloon.)
3. From the list of training activities successfully complete a further eleven items from at least five of the sections.

PRACTICAL SKILLS

1. Build and fly a model glider (to fly for five seconds if hand launched).
2. Build and fly a rubber-powered model (to fly for at least 15 seconds) or a jetex-powered model.
3. Build and fly a hot air balloon or a kite.
4. Build and fly a control-line model aircraft, to make at least three circuits **or** build a non-flying demonstration model with working controls.
5. Build and fly a radio-controlled model aircraft (this may be undertaken with other Scouts).
6. Build a scale model aircraft to a satisfactory standard (plastic kit permitted).
7. Build a scale model from photographs or plans, or by modifying a standard kit to produce a different but authentic version of the aircraft.
8. Undertake a project to demonstrate a particular aeronautical principle and build a suitable model to illustrate it.
9. Organise a visit to an airfield and arrange a suitable programme for a group of Scouts.
10. Have had sufficient dual instruction to be able to fly a glider or light aircraft from take-off around a circuit and position for landing to the satisfaction of the accompanying qualified instructor.
11. Any other one activity of a similar nature and level of achievement as agreed by the Patrol Leaders' Council.

FLIGHT SAFETY AND AIRMANSHIP

12. List the main types of aircraft.
13. Name the main control surfaces of an aeroplane, explain how they work and how they are controlled.
14. Know the rules in *Policy, Organisation and Rules* relating to flying, and fly in a light aircraft or glider as a passenger.
15. Assist a light aircraft pilot in his duties before and after a flight (for example, moving aircraft, strapping in, starting up, picketing).
16. Assist a glider pilot with ground handling and launching his aircraft, and be able to assist after a field landing.
17. Assist a balloon pilot in his duties before and after a flight (for example, unpacking, inflating, recovery after a flight).
18. Explain the duties of an aircraft marshaller and be able to demonstrate marshalling signals.
19. Arrange for a suitably experienced instructor to train you in how a parachute works. Be able to put on a parachute harness and demonstrate the correct landing roll.
20. Explain how an aircraft lifejacket works and be able to demonstrate its use.
21. Assist with the launching and recovery of a paraglider. Make two ascents, without release.
22. Explain the procedure for inter-airfield flights. Prepare a flight plan in draft on behalf of a pilot.
23. Any other one activity of a similar nature and level of achievement as agreed by the Patrol Leaders' Council.

continued overleaf . . .

AIRCRAFT RECOGNITION AND OPERATIONS

24. Identify, either from pictures or in flight, 12 aircraft in common use today:
    four civil commercial aircraft;
    four military aircraft;
    four light private aircraft.
25. Identify 20 aircraft from pictures seen for not more than ten seconds each, the aircraft being selected from the list published by Headquarters for this purpose.
26. Identify 40 aircraft from pictures seen for not more than ten seconds each, the aircraft being selected from the list published by Headquarters for this purpose.
27. Identify the nationality of ten different aircraft from their markings, selected from the list published by Headquarters for this purpose.
28. Describe at least six airlines by their names and markings. Identify their home countries and main bases.
29. Identify at least six airlines by name and describe six routes operated by each, together with the aircraft used.
30. Plan a journey to a destination on the other side of the world, giving airline, aircraft, date and time of departure, en route stops and date and time of arrival (local time) with flying elapsed times.
31. Discuss the design characteristics of a chosen aircraft in relation to its operational role.
32. Discuss the problem of aerospace flight including acceleration to escape velocity, the reason for weightlessness and re-entry problems.
33. Demonstrate a general knowledge of the progress of space exploration, describing in particular one space programme.
34. Demonstrate the scale of the solar system with a drawing or model to show the relative positions of the planets.
35. Any other one activity of a similar nature and level of achievement as agreed by the Patrol Leaders' Council.

NAVIGATION

36. Identify the conventional signs in use on air maps.
37. Explain the workings and errors of an aircraft compass.
38. Explain the workings of aircraft pressure instruments (altimeter, air speed indicator and so on) and the sources of errors.
39. For a cross-country flight of at least 80 kilometres, work out the time of flight (overhead starting point to overhead destination) for a given airspeed, assuming (a) a given headwind, (b) a given tailwind.
40. Given a heading and track, work out the type and amount of drift. Establish the wind velocity given track and groundspeed, course and airspeed.
41. For a cross-country flight of at least 80 kilometres, determine a heading given a track, windspeed and direction.
42. Demonstrate how the 1 in 60 rule is used for correcting track errors. Demonstrate how the distance marks and five or ten degree lines may be used to correct estimated time of arrival and track errors.
43. Illustrate, by simple diagrams, latitude and longitude. Explain the need for different types of map projections.

44. Illustrate by simple diagram how a fix can be obtained from two position lines. Describe briefly two ways in which bearings can be obtained in an aircraft so position lines can be drawn on a chart.
45. Any other one activity of a similar nature and level of achievement as agreed by the Patrol Leaders' Council.

METEOROLOGY

46. Explain the flight conditions which can be expected in various cloud formations and weather conditions.
47. Explain how temperature and pressure are measured, list the units used and demonstrate conversion between these units by use of tables and scales of calculation.
48. Identify the weather conditions associated with the movement of air masses over the United Kingdom (Polar/Tropical, Maritime/ Continental).
49. Identify the weather associated with frontal systems in the United Kingdom and be able to explain the meaning of the terms used in describing a weather map (col, ridge, trough, occlusion and so on).
50. Interpret a weather map (synoptic chart) and identify at least two natural signs for weather changes in your area. Set up a simple weather station and keep a log book of your recordings over a period of one month.
51. Explain the effect of weather conditions on navigation, for example, drift, Buys Ballots' Law, air speed and altimeter errors, changes of wind directions and speed with height or at fronts.
52. Explain how readings of upper air conditions are obtained.
53. Explain the danger of icing to aircraft and the conditions giving rise to this phenomenon.
54. Any other one activity of a similar nature and level of achievement as agreed by the Patrol Leaders' Council.

AERO ENGINES

55. List the basic types of piston aero engines and identify the main components of a piston engine.
56. Explain the basic principles of a piston engine, including the four stroke cycle with consideration of valve and ignition timing.
57. Explain the effect of altitude on a piston engine, with particular respect to mixture control, carburettor icing and the use of hot air.
58. Explain the purpose of variable pitch and constant-speed propellers.
59. Discuss the theory of propeller design, including limits of blade size and speed, blade numbers and shape, contra-rotating props and so on.
60. Explain how thrust is obtained by jets or rockets and explain the principle of ramjets.
61. Explain the principles of a jet engine (centrifugal or axial compressor types) and identify the main components of such an engine.
62. Discuss the relative merits of piston engines, turbojets, turboprops, turbofans, ramjets and rockets.
63. Identify the main types of aircraft fuels and fuel systems.
64. Demonstrate a knowledge of the fuel systems used in space rockets or missiles and the means of control when outside the earth's atmosphere.
65. Any other one activity of a similar nature and level of achievement as agreed by the Patrol Leaders' Council.

continued overleaf . . .

COMMUNICATIONS AND AIR TRAFFIC CONTROL

66. Identify the signals used on the airfield signals square, together with runway and airfield markings.
67. Identify the lamp and pyrotechnic signals used on an airfield.
68. Recite the phonetic alphabet.
69. Use the Morse code to identify lights and radio beacons.
70. Explain the system of controlled airspace and the air traffic control organisation in the United Kingdom.
71. Demonstrate the R/T procedure for a simple cross-country flight. Explain the distress procedure.
72. Demonstrate a knowledge of the main aircraft navigational aids and systems with special reference to their use by private pilots.
73. Explain the basic principles of radar and its main uses in aviation.
74. Explain the right of way rules for different types of aircraft and for aircraft on converging courses.
75. Demonstrate a knowledge of navigation lights, instrument flying condition and the quadrantal height rule.
76. Demonstrate examples of the ground-to-air emergency code.
77. Any other one activity of a similar nature and level of achievement as agreed by the Patrol Leaders' Council.

PRINCIPLES OF FLIGHT

78. Explain how a wing gives lift and detail factors affecting lift and the causes of stalling.
79. Explain the relationships between lift and drag, thrust and weight.
80. Explain the meaning of trim and the importance of weight and balance.
81. Demonstrate an ability to trim a suitable model glider to perform a straight glide, stall and dive and specified turn.
82. List the forces acting on a glider and explain how soaring flight is obtained (thermals and wave lift).
83. Explain the purpose and operation of flaps, slots and slats.
84. Explain how basic aerobatic manoeuvres are carried out.
85. Demonstrate a knowledge of the principles of take-off and landing with special reference to light aircraft.
86. Demonstrate a knowledge of the special problems of supersonic flight.
87. Explain the main methods by which short or vertical take-off can be achieved.
88. Demonstrate a knowledge of the basic principles of helicopters and how they are controlled.
89. Explain the difference between ground speed and air speed and how wind is used to aid take-off and landing.
90. Describe the air-flow around a modern square parachute, explaining how it develops lift and how it is controlled.
91. Any other one activity of a similar nature and level of achievement as agreed by the Patrol Leaders' Council.

Air Researcher

Pursuit

1. Know the safety rules as laid down in *Policy, Organisation and Rules.*
2. Carry out a research project over a period of at least three months into one of the following subjects:
   (a) The development of aircraft over one of the following periods:
      (i) 1783 to 1904;
      (ii) 1904 to 1918;
      (iii) 1918 to 1933;
      (iv) 1933 to 1945;
      (v) 1945 to 1960;
      (vi) 1960 to 1975;
      (vii) 1975 to the present.
   (b) The development of balloons of all types.
   (c) The development of rockets, including man carrying types.
   (d) The development of the jet engine.

In the course of your research, visit at least one place of interest which is directly relevant to your project, for example a museum, an air display or a factory.

The presentation of your project must include a model which you have made to illustrate some aspect of your research. Other support material such as sketches, diagrams, slides and cuttings should be used wherever possible.

Air Spotter

Pursuit

1. Identify from photographs or silhouettes shown for ten seconds each, three-quarters of the aircraft in the list published by Headquarters for this purpose.
2. Keep a log for three months reporting aircraft seen, giving identities or recognition features, approximate headings, times, dates and so on.
3. *Either:*
   (a) Recognise and name national aircraft markings, both service and civil, of at least six countries including the United Kingdom.

   Or:
   (b) Understand the R.A.F. system of letter designation according to aircraft function and give examples of three such designations.

   Or:
   (c) Name three basic training aircraft used in private flying. Give a brief report on one, naming a club and airfield where it is used (local wherever possible).
4. Describe the recognition features of six aircraft selected by the examiner.

Angler

Interest

1. Know the water safety rules. Understand the dangers of wading in fresh water and shore fishing in the sea and the precautions to be taken.
2. Go fishing in fresh or salt water on at least six occasions in three months. Keep a record of, or discuss with the examiner, these fishing trips showing numbers, species and size of fish caught, method, tackle and bait used, weather and water conditions.
3. Know the dates of the fresh water closed seasons and size limits of salt and/or fresh water fish in the area(s) in which you fish.
4. (a) Be able to identify one of the following groups of species:

   Either:

   (i) bass, cod and grey mullet.

   Or:

   (ii) roach, perch, pike, common carp and tench.

   Or:

   (iii) brown trout, rainbow trout and salmon.

   (b) Have a knowledge of the habitat and feeding behaviour of the fish identified and know suitable baits, flies, lures and hook sizes.

   (c) Know how to handle a fish when landing it and how to despatch a sea or game fish.
5. *Either:*

   Cast with beach fishing tackle a measured 45 metres.

   Or:

   Cast ledger and float tackle into a 1 metre circle at least three times out of six at 9 metres range.

   Or:

   Cast a trout fly on a fly line 11 metres reasonably accurately and with a minimum of splashing.
6. Identify:

   Either:

   (a) A pike plug, pike or perch spoon, wet and dry trout flies, a salmon fly (standard pattern or tube fly).

   Or:

   (b) A commonly used terminal rig for sea fish ledgering.

Artist

Interest

1. Paint or draw an illustration of a scene from a story selected by the examiner.
2. Paint or draw **either** a person from life **or** an object set before you.
3. Paint or draw a landscape set by, or known to, the examiner.
4. Show the examiner a selection of your recent work.

Astronomer

Pursuit

1. Recognise the prominent constellations visible throughout the year.

   Winter: Orion, Aries, Auriga, Taurus (Pleiades and Hyades), Canis Major, Canis Minor.
   Spring: Leo, Bootes.
   Summer: Cygnus, Lyra, Aquila, Delphinus.
   Autumn: Pegasus and the Circumpolar constellations of Ursa Major and Cassiopeia.
2. Recognise and show an elementary knowledge of the following stars:

   Winter: Sirius, Procyon, Betelgeux, Saiph, Rigel, Alderbaran, Hamal, Capella.
   Summer: Deneb, Vega, Altair.
   Autumn: Merak, Dubhe.
3. Keep a diary of your observations through the year, which should include sightings of meteor showers, changes of planetary positions and eclipses.
4. Know the meanings of elementary astronomical terms such as axial rotation, synodic and sidereal periods, opposition, conjunction, meridian, ecliptic, celestial equator.
5. Give a general description of the Solar System, the individual Planets and the Galaxy.
6. Know about landings made or planned on other bodies in the Solar System since 1969 and about man's activities in space.
7. In addition to the observations made in your diary, keep a record of these activities during the year in question and say how these will contribute towards future space missions.

Athlete

Interest

Compete in any three events (two track and one field or vice versa) and gain points as indicated on the scoring chart which appears below.

Minimum points total for award of badge:

Age	Points (female)	Points (male)
Under 11	8	9
Under 12	10	11
Under 13	12	13
Under 14	13	15
Under 15	15	16
Under 16	16	17

Notes:

(i) Scouts who have gained the Three Star Award of the British Athletics Federation relevant to their age qualify automatically for this badge.

(ii) Scoring tables for the British Athletics Federation Five Star Award Scheme relevant to the physically handicapped can be obtained from the British Athletics Federation, Edgbaston House, 3 Duchess Place, Hagley Road, Edgbaston, Birmingham, B16 8NM.

(iii) The recommended weights of the shot, discus and cricket ball are 4 kg, 1kg and 0.135kg respectively.

Points	100 Mtrs	200 Mtrs	400 Mtrs	800 Mtrs	1500 Mtrs	High Jump	Long Jump	Shot	Discus	Cricket Ball
	Sec	*Sec*	*Sec*	*Min*	*Min*	*Min*	*Mtr*	*Mtr*	*Mtr*	*Mtr*
10	11.2	23.1	51.8	2.06	4.12	1.81	5.70	11.6	39.00	-
9	11.7	24.3	56.0	2.12	4.32	1.71	5.00	9.7	31.50	-
8	12.6	26.5	61.0	2.22	4.57	1.56	4.50	8.2	26.00	65.00
7	13.6	29.5	66.0	2.34	5.27	1.36	4.00	6.8	21.00	55.00
6	14.6	32.5	71.0	2.54	5.57	1.18	3.50	5.8	17.60	45.00
5	15.6	34.5	76.0	3.14	6.27	1.08	3.04	4.9	14.60	35.00
4	16.6	36.6	84.0	3.34	7.10	.98	2.73	4.4	11.50	30.00
3	17.6	38.6	94.0	3.54	8.00	.88	2.43	3.8	7.25	25.00
2	18.6	40.6	108.0	4.14	8.50	.78	2.13	2.2	4.75	20.00
1	30.3	45.0	135.0	5.00	9.40	.68	1.70	1.8	3.25	15.00

Bellringer

Pursuit

To gain the badge you must complete all the requirements in one of the following alternatives:

A 1. Ring rounds correctly, treble and inside bell.
2. Raise and lower a bell.
3. Ring one standard method on an inside bell or ring not less than 30 call changes without fault.
4. Explain the technical terms used in ringing in your own tower.
5. Describe the parts of a bell and how it is rung, and show that you understand the importance of rope maintenance.
6. Explain, in general terms, how a church bell is made and tuned.
7. Attend regularly at your own tower for service ringing and practise for at least three months.

B 1. Be a regular member of a handbell team, either at school, in your Scout Group or other organisation for a period of at least three months.
2. Take part in a stage presentation.
3. Know how to care for a set of handbells.
4. Be able to read music appropriate for handbell ringing and translate this through a good striking technique.

C 1. Know the names and functions of various parts of a handbell.
2. Be capable of ringing any two handbells in both 'rounds' and 'call changes', maintaining a good striking performance.
3. Ring the trebles for a Plain Hunt to a maximum of eight bells.
4. *Either:*

   Ring the trebles for a touch of 120 with No. 2 as an inside bell working in a standard method.

   Or:

   Ring the tenors for a touch of 120 of a standard method with the leading tenor (such as 5 or 7), working as an inside bell.

   Or:

   Ring two inside bells for a plain course in a standard method of more than five bells - minor, triples or major.
5. Explain in general terms how a handbell is made and tuned.
6. Write out plain courses of at least two standard methods or show a knowledge of these methods.

Note:

Examiners may make appropriate amendments to A in respect of carillon bells.

Boatswain

Pursuit

1. (a) Have a general knowledge of ropes, including different uses, stresses and strains, and demonstrate the correct methods of stowing cables, coiling light lines and painters.

   (b) Have a knowledge of sail canvas and Terylene, be able to name the parts of a sail and know how to maintain sails in good condition.

   (c) Have a good knowledge of both standing and running rigging in:

   (i) an open sailing craft;

   (ii) a gaff-rigged vessel;

   (iii) a class racing boat.

   (d) Have a practical knowledge of at least three types of purchase tackles.

   (e) Demonstrate that you can heave a lifeline 18 metres with reasonable accuracy.

2. (a) Be able to use a palm and needle and make a drogue with canvas.

   (b) Make a rope fender for a dinghy.

   (c) Make a grommet and a stopper knot ready for operational use in a sailing boat.

   (d) Complete a long splice or make up a pair of lizards using bull's eyes or thimbles.

   (e) Demonstrate in a sailing boat whilst underway the following:

   single catspaw, running bowline, double sheetbend and mouse a hook.

3. Take a regular and practical part in one of the following activities:

   (a) Constructing a canoe.

   (b) Constructing a hard chine boat.

   (c) Carrying out hull repairs to a wood, fibreglass or plastic boat.

   (d) Making a spinnaker or stormsail.

4. Take a responsible part in one of the following activities:

   (a) Rig a derrick (or derricks) with rope, spars and tackles and so on, and lift a small dinghy from the water.

   (b) Rig a form of breeches buoy, using a lifebuoy, ropes, tackles and spars and so on, and demonstrate its use.

   (c) Launch a boat from a sandy or shingle foreshore, beach the craft and haul it up well clear of the water. The rigging of a hull strop and the use of a carrick bend should feature in the hauling-up evolution.

5. Take a leading part in one of the following exercises afloat:

   (a) Board a sailing boat, apparently dismasted, stream a drogue and ride it, construct and hoist a jury rig, recover the drogue and sail the boat home, with the candidate taking the helm. The jury rig must include one makeshift mast, two jury sails, a rolling hitch, single catspaw, sheetbend and appropriate lashings. The distance of the operation out and in should be approximately 900 metres (4 cables) each leg.

Notes:

(i) One orthodox sail may be utilised but not in its normal or proper setting.

(ii) In craft carrying two masts, one orthodox mast may be retained to set one jury sail.

(iii) The second jury sail is to be fashioned from available materials, for example oilskins, canvas covers, sacking, tarpaulins and so on.

(b) Answer a signal for assistance from a sailing boat with a 'damaged rudder' and 'aground in shallow water' at approximately 900 metres (4 cables) distant. Refloat the craft by warping off, rig for sailing, recover ground tackle and sail the boat home. The candidate to board the 'stranded' craft, supervise laying out of kedge anchor and warping off, recovery of anchor and re-rigging of sailing gear. The candidate should sail the craft home using a steering oar in place of the 'damaged' rudder.

Notes:

(i) The candidate should muster the crew with the appropriate pipe.

(ii) The candidate should supervise preparation of the pulling or power boat with the appropriate gear to include: warp, spare anchor and a drogue.

Camp Cook

Interest

1. Discuss with the examiner how and where to shop for food and how to transport it.
2. Demonstrate proper storage and cooking under camp conditions. This must include knowledge about food poisoning and hygiene in the camp kitchen.
3. Cook without utensils, but using foil, a two-course meal for yourself and at least one other person.
4. Successfully cook and serve a breakfast of your own choice such as:
   bacon and eggs;
   scrambled eggs;
   sausages with tomatoes;
   kippers;
   porridge.
5. Successfully cook and serve a 'main course' dish of your choice such as:
   a stew with dumplings;
   a mixed grill;
   chicken Maryland.
6. Successfully cook and serve a sweet of your own choice such as:
   a steamed or boiled pudding;
   stewed fruit and custard;
   fruit fritters.
7. Draw up two menus (including quantities) of three courses each (not all of which need or require cooking) for a Patrol of six.

Notes:

(i) All dishes to be cooked under camp conditions and preferably on a wood fire.

(ii) Cultural and vegetarian dishes can be included in requirements 3, 4, 5, 6 or 7.

Camper

Pursuit

1. Have camped under canvas with a Troop or Patrol for a total of not less than 15 nights.
2. Pitch and strike a hike tent.
3. Direct successfully the pitching, striking and packing of a Patrol tent.
4. Know what to look for when choosing a campsite.
5. Show an understanding of the principles of camp hygiene and the importance of order and cleanliness in camp generally.
6. Demonstrate how to store food in a quartermaster's tent.
7. Construct alone a camp larder, a camp oven and two other gadgets of your own choice.
8. At a camp, cook for yourself and at least one other - but not more than a normal Patrol - **either** a hot breakfast meal **or** a dish for a main meal which must include two vegetables.
9. Have a good knowledge of *Scout Camping.*

Camp Warden

Service

1. Have camped on ten separate occasions on at least four different sites.
2. Have worked for at least seven days at a permanent (District, County/Area or National) Scout campsite, helping the Warden(s) to their satisfaction.
3. Explain, and where possible demonstrate, the daily maintenance required for campsite equipment.
4. Explain, and where possible demonstrate, four of the following:
   (a) The importance of having clean toilets, both from a health point of view and to maintain the image of the site.
   (b) The procedure to prevent burst pipes during the winter time and the steps to take when pipes do burst.
   (c) The procedure for unblocking a blocked drain.
   (d) The need for good drainage, keeping ditches clear and so on.
   (e) Refuse disposal and how this can be operated to maximise the retention of recylable materials.
   (f) The need to respect wildlife alongside the needs and requirements of campers, for example, leaving a strip of long grass around field edges to encourage insect life, establishment of copses and the planting of new trees.
   (g) The increased use of computers in campsite management.
5. Have a good knowledge of *Scout Camping.*
6. Become familiar with an activity run on site and explain the use and maintenance of equipment used for that activity.
7. Demonstrate the ability to use three of the following:
   (a) Felling axe;
   (b) Bush saw;
   (c) Maul;
   (d) Two man cross cut saw;
   (e) Pruning tool;
   (f) Sickle;
   (g) Hand tools, for example, hammer and chisel, wood saw, hack saw and so on.
8. Discuss with the examiner developments and improvements you would like to see on any permanent campsite with which you are familiar.

Elementary Canoeist

Interest

1. Qualify for the British Canoe Union One Star Test.
2. Take part in a canoeing activity with other Scouts.

Notes:

(i) A Scout who gains a similar BCU qualification at an equivalent level, qualifies automatically for requirement one of this badge.

(ii) In brief summary the one star test includes launching, forward and backward paddling, stopping in both directions, sweep strokes, disembarking, capsize drill. It also includes a simple theory section and other stroke principles. Further details are available from either the Activity office at Gilwell Park or BCU, Mapperly Hall, Lucknow Avenue, Nottingham N93 5FA - Tel: 0115 982 1100.

Canoeist

Pursuit

1. Qualify for the British Canoe Union Two Star Test.
2. Take part in a canoeing activity with other Scouts.

Notes:

(i) A Scout who gains a similar BCU qualification at an equivalent level qualifies automatically for requirement one of this badge.

(ii) In brief summary the two star test includes basic skills plus support and draw strokes, brace turns, capsize and rescue techniques and stern rudder. It also includes a theory section and the principles of sculling and eskimo rolls. Further details are available from the Activity Office at Gilwell Park or BCU at Mapperly Hall, Lucknow Avenue, Nottingham N93 5FA - Tel: 0115 982 1100.

Advanced Canoeist

Pursuit

1. Qualify for the British Canoe Union Three Star Test.
2. Take part in a canoeing activity with other Scouts.

Notes:

(i) A Scout who gains a similar BCU qualification at an equivalent level qualifies automatically for requirement 1 of this badge.

(ii) In brief summary the Three Star Test includes basic skills plus sculling, support and draw strokes, recovery strokes, Eskimo rescues, Eskimo rolls and single handed rescues. It also includes a theory section containing the principles of towing and personal equipment needed for a day on the water. Futher details are available from the Activities office at Gilwell Park or BCU at Mapperly Hall, Lucknow Avenue, Nottingham N93 5FA - Tel: 0115 982 1100.

Caver

Interest

1. Maintain a log of the exploration on at least four different trips in at least two different cave systems as a member of a properly led group.
2. Keep a record of these trips, including sketch maps of the systems and the routes followed.
3. Have a knowledge of the contents of the caving and cave conservation codes.

Note:

Caving and pot holing are potentially hazardous pursuits and Scouts should only undertake this badge if they can gain the necessary experience as a member of a properly organised caving group, run by experienced adult cavers, who will directly supervise any vertical pitches.

Communicator

Interest

To gain the badge you must complete all the requirements in one of the following alternatives:

A 1. (a) Log 25 different amateur radio stations showing details of date, time, call sign, frequency, readability and location. (Some broadcast stations may be included.)

(b) Demonstrate how to tune a simple communications receiver.

(c) Give an example of a typical 'greetings message'.

2. Know the more commonly used HF and VHF amateur frequency bands and explain in simple terms how radio waves travel around the world.

3. (a) Know the international phonetic alphabet and define at least eight international Q code signals.

(b) Demonstrate your ability to recognise call signs from the UK and near continent.

4. Visit an amateur radio station.

5. Understand the regulations governing the use of amateur radio equipment.

B Pass the Radio Amateur Novice Licence A or B.

continued overleaf . . .

C 1. Send and receive a short message by Morse code or Semaphore at a rate of five words per minute.

2. Demonstrate that you know a recognised procedure when sending and receiving a message.

3. Know the international phonetic alphabet and define at least eight international Q code signals.

4. Construct a simple Morse code oscillator and send a short message to the examiner.

D 1. (a) Log 25 different citizens' band users contacted showing details of date, time identification, signal strength, readability and location.

(b) Discuss with the examiner your experiences in keeping the log, for example, use of equipment and effect of various conditions on range of reception.

(c) Demonstrate the use of citizens' band equipment by making a contact with another citizens' band user and maintaining the contact for at least two minutes.

2. Discuss with the examiner the DTI recommended Code of Practice and the reasons for reserving certain channels for specific functions.

3. Demonstrate a knowledge of the 'ten codes' used and discuss their advantages and disadvantages.

4. Show a working knowledge of the conditions under which a DTI Citizens Band Licence is issued, how suitable equipment may be recognised and the restrictions on its use. Demonstrate that all equipment used conforms with these regulations.

5. Discuss with the examiner the cause of radio and television interference and the steps that might be taken to minimise the effects.

E Pass the restricted Certificate of Competence in (Marine) Radio Telephony (VHF only).

Community

Service

To gain the badge you must pass all the requirements in one of the following alternatives:

A 1. Find out about local community services (for example health, education, leisure, social) using such resources as the local authority, youth officers and local library. Discuss with the Patrol Leaders' Council how these services meet the needs of the members of the community.

2. Carry out a study of one aspect of community concern in your area after consulting the Patrol Leaders' Council and Scout Leader. The study should be of approximately six months' duration, and could include the old, the young, the disabled, the lonely or the unemployed.

3. Take a regular part in a form of service to the community, spread over at least two months. Explain to the Patrol Leaders' Council what you have learned from this experience of social involvement.

B You must discuss this option with the examiner before undertaking any of the requirements.

1. With a friend, push and be pushed in a wheelchair around your neighbourhood, visiting shops and public buildings. Describe your experience to the examiner.

2. Show how to open and close a wheelchair properly and how to take it up and down curbs, down a slope and up and down stairs.

3. Demonstrate the techniques of lifting someone who has a weakness in the legs and of transferring them from one chair to another.

4. Assemble a display of not less than eight items of aids used by people with special needs. Explain to your Patrol and the examiner how these items are used.

5. Learn the following Makaton phrases - Hello, Please, Thank you, Friend, Help, Home, Tired, Eat, Drink, Yes, No, O.K., Wash, Toilet and Goodbye.

6. Help to make a Special Needs Awareness Trail for the Scouts in your Patrol. Take part in it yourself. Tell your examiner about it.

7. *Either:*

   (a) Spend a total of 15 hours within a period of three months either helping at a PHAB Club or Gateway Club or helping at a special Pack or Troop which caters for Scouts with special needs.

   Or:

   (b) Help at a camp at which there are a number of Scouts with special needs.

   Or:

   (c) Any other one activity of a similar nature and level of achievement as agreed by the Patrol Leaders' Council.

continued overleaf . . .

8. Discuss with the Patrol Leaders' Council and with the examiner how you now feel about people with special needs and how you will behave towards them in the future.

C *Either:*

1. Take part in a visit to a local police station and find out about:
   (a) The organisation of a police force and the rank structure.
   (b) The various specialist departments.
   (c) Communications including personal radio, emergency system and phonetic alphabet.
   (d) The practical side of preventing and detecting crime.
2. Show an understanding of crime prevention in the home and the community.
3. Observe a stranger for a period of two minutes and, after a period of time, be able to describe him or her in such a manner as to enable the person to be recognised.
4. Show a good knowledge of the Highway Code.

Or:

Take part in a locally organised course as agreed by your Patrol Leaders' Council, Scout Leader and the police force.

Cook

Pursuit

1. Discuss with the examiner how and where to shop for food and how to transport it.
2. Demonstrate proper storage and cooking. This must include knowledge about food poisoning and hygiene in the kitchen.
3. Know what is meant by normal culinary terms, for example au gratin, roux, to sweat, fold, render.
4. Prepare successfully two of the following sauces: Mornay, Apple, Mustard, Parsley, Hollandaise, Mint.
5. Prepare and cook by yourself two of the following:

   Shepherd's Pie;
   Yorkshire Pudding;
   Fruit Cake;
   Plain Omelette;
   Apple Tart;
   Macaroni Cheese.
6. Cook and serve, for two to four people, two main course dishes and two sweets demonstrating the necessary preparation and serving skills.
7. Demonstrate four different ways of cooking potatoes (for example baked in jacket, creamed, croquettes, lyonnaise and so on).
8. Plan a varied menu for yourself for one week and discuss your choices with the examiner.

Notes:

(i) At least one of the dishes selected for requirements 5 and 6 to be cooked under camp conditions.

(ii) Cultural and vegetarian dishes can be included in requirement 5 or 6.

Craft

Interest

The project to be completed for this badge must be agreed with the examiner beforehand and should last approximately six hours.

From your own design, make an object or objects, from materials such as wood, metal, clay, plastic, leather or the like. The design should include details of construction.

Cyclist

Interest

1. Own, or have used satisfactorily for at least six months, a bicycle properly equipped and in good working order.
2. Be able to make simple adjustments and repairs at the discretion of the examiner, for example change a tyre and tube, mend a puncture, replace a brake shoe and block, adjust the height of the saddle and the handlebar to enable a younger Scout to ride the bicycle.
3. Demonstrate that you know and observe the *Highway Code,* traffic signals, lighting-up times, road signs, national system of road numbering and direction and that you can read a road map.
4. Take part in a Scout activity which includes the use of bicycles.

Notes:

(i) Cycle helmets should be worn at all times during cycling activities.

(ii) A Scout who has passed the National Cycling Proficiency Test of the Royal Society for the Prevention of Accidents or the Cycleway National Course in Cycling Awareness qualifies automatically for those parts of requirements 2 and 3 which are covered by these courses.

Advanced Cyclist

Pursuit

A On Road

1. Hold the Cyclist Badge.
2. Demonstrate an ability to carry out small general repairs, including at least four of the following, to the satisfaction of the examiner:
   (a) Replacement of a brake cable;
   (b) Replacement of a worn chain;
   (c) Replacement of a broken spoke;
   (d) Removal and replacement of cranks or pedals;
   (e) Adjustment of bearings and gears.
3. Explain to the examiner what extra precautions should be taken when cycling in the dark or in wet weather conditions (including lights, reflectors, dynamos, and the additional time needed by those in motor vehicles to stop in the wet).
4. Demonstrate the ability to control a cycle through a slalom course.
5. Show an understanding of *The Highway Code* as it relates to cyclists (including road signs and helmets).
6. Have a basic knowledge of first aid and what to do in the case of accidents.
7. Have a sound knowledge of map reading, being able to estimate distances, identify countryside features and terrain and orientate a map using local geography and a compass.
8. Plan and carry out an all day ride of not less than 40km (25 miles).

B Off Road

1. Hold the Cyclist Badge.
2. Demonstrate an ability to carry out small general repairs, including at least four of the following, to the satisfaction of the examiner:
   (a) Replacement of a brake cable;
   (b) Replacement of a worn chain;
   (c) Replacement of a broken spoke;
   (d) Removal and replacement of cranks or pedals;
   (e) Adjustment of bearings and gears.
3. Have an understanding of The Scout Association's Rules for taking part in adventurous activities.
4. Demonstrate an understanding of the Mountain Bike Code of Conduct.
5. Demonstrate the ability to control the cycle over different types of terrain.
6. Show an understanding of the damage that may be caused to the environment through careless cycling across the countryside.
7. Have a basic knowledge of first aid including the treatment of hypothermia and know what to do in the case of an accident.
8. Have a sound knowledge of map reading, being able to estimate distances, identify countryside features and terrain and orientate a map using local geography and a compass.
9. Plan and carry out an all day ride of not less than 30 km (20 miles).

Note:

Cycle helmets should be worn at all times during cycling activities.

D.I.Y.

Service

Demonstrate any six of the following of your own choice:

(a) Renew a sash cord, or replace a casement window frame and hang it.

(b) Glaze windows, both in wood and iron frames.

(c) Help to paint and paper a room.

(d) Take precautions to prevent frozen pipes in a house.

(e) Repair defective plastering.

(f) Re-hang a door and repair door furniture, including handles, locks and so on.

(g) Effect minor repairs to furniture, such as broken castors and minor upholstery repairs.

(h) Help to lay a pavement.

(i) Put a neat patch on a garment.

(j) Clean and polish a car.

(k) Repair a gate or fence.

(l) Mix concrete and effect simple repairs with it.

(m) Repair children's toys.

(n) Lay linoleum.

(o) Replace a tap washer.

(p) Oil and adjust a lawn mower.

(q) The immediate steps to be taken in the case of a burst water pipe.

Note:

Other options can be chosen by yourself in consultation with the badge examiner.

Electronics

Pursuit

1. (a) Be able to recognise common electronic components which are shown to you by the Examiner. Explain, in simple terms, the functions that they usually perform in electronic circuits.
   (b) Understand the systems used for marking components with their values and be able to identify the values of resistors and capacitors so marked. Understand the importance of the rating of a component.
   (c) Know the symbols that are used to represent common components in circuit diagrams. Show how to identify the polarity of a diode and a specific pin number on an integrated circuit.
2. Demonstrate a knowledge of safe working practices to be followed when handling electronic components, working with electronic circuits and when soldering.
3. Use a multimeter to measure voltage, current and resistance in a simple circuit. Discuss with the Examiner the relationship between these values.
4. Discuss with the Examiner the main differences in operation of digital and analogue circuits.
5. (a) Construct three simple circuits, one of which should be based mainly on digital electronics. These may be from a book or magazine, or circuits that you have designed yourself. At least one of the circuits should be soldered, using either strip-board or a custom made printed circuit board.
   (b) Explain to the Examiner the principles behind the operation of each circuit and the typical values of voltage and current found in each.

Emergency Aid

Service

Qualify for one of the following:

(a) The Essentials of First Aid Certificate of the St. John Ambulance Association.

(b) The Junior Certificate of the St. Andrew's Ambulance Association.

(c) The Youth First Aid Certificate of the British Red Cross Society.

Entertainer

Collective Achievement

To gain this badge you must pass all the requirements in one of the following alternatives:

A Carry out these activities as a member of a group of Scouts, preferably as a Patrol project.

1. Write and plan a short entertainment with your Patrol or group. This could take the form of a sketch, film or slide and tape presentation, camp fire or stage routine involving some of the following: mime, drama, music, storytelling, conjuring, photography, sound recording.
2. Prepare your entertainment, ensuring that everyone has a job to do, for example actor, producer, stage manager, publicity manager.
3. Present your entertainment at a Pack or Troop Parents' Evening.
4. Discuss with your Scout Leader, or other adult (see Note ii) the value of the work you have undertaken.

B 1. Take an active part in a District or County/Area Scout show. This should require a minimum of two months regular rehearsing.

2. Discuss with your Scout Leader, or other adult (see Note ii) the value of the work you have undertaken.

Notes:

(i) Alternative activities may be undertaken as agreed by the Patrol Leaders' Council after consultation with the badge examiner.

(ii) An adult with some expertise in stage entertainment may be consulted to help with the selection of projects and preparation of alternatives.

Explorer

Pursuit

1. Arrange and carry out an expedition for yourself and at least three other Scouts, preferably members of your Patrol, of not less than two days' and one night's duration, in country not previously visited (see Note i).
2. Plan a project and submit it to the examiner for approval. Carry it out alone or with a companion, to the examiner's satisfaction. The type of project should be a simple exploration, such as identifying and mapping all footpaths, bridle paths or waterways within a 1.5 kilometre radius of a given point.
3. Complete a journey, with a companion, of five kilometres by compass bearings only. Six different bearings by degrees are to be used. You may use a map.

Notes:

(i) The expedition may be carried out on foot, by cycle, on horseback, by canoe or by boat. All equipment and food for the expedition is to be carried by those taking part.

(ii) Cycle helmets should be worn at all times during cycling activities.

Fire Safety

Service

1. Understand how your local fire service works.
2. Give a simple explanation of the process of combustion. Know the effects of smoke and heat, and how to act in smoke.
3. Know the dangers and understand the fire precautions necessary in the home relating to:
   (a) oil heaters and open solid fuel fires;
   (b) portable electric fires;
   (c) airing linen;
   (d) electric wiring and fuses;
   (e) smoking materials particularly matches;
   (f) uses of household gas and petrol;
   (g) party decorations;
   (h) doors and windows;
   (i) candles.
4. Explain the benefits from having smoke detectors in the home and describe where they should be located.
5. Know the dangers of fire at camp and what precautions should be taken. Know the causes of heath and grass fires and how to deal with an outbreak.
6. Explain what action should be taken, and why, on an outbreak of fire. Know the various methods of calling the fire service and the correct procedure to be followed. Know what happens from the time of the call to its acceptance by the fire service and the reasons for such action.
7. Know how to use and recognise various fire extinguishers including water, dry powder, foam and carbon dioxide types. Know what kinds of fire they should be used on. Know how to deal with a person whose clothes are on fire.
8. Be proficient in making a chair knot and bowline. Explain the methods of rescue employed and explain and demonstrate crawling with an insensible person.

Forester

Pursuit

1. Be able to identify in summer and in winter the following trees: Oak, Ash, Sycamore, Beech, Elm, Birch, Horse Chestnut, Lime, Plane, Field Maple, Spruce and Pine. Know how to identify any tree by reference to identification keys.
2. Have a knowledge of the tending of woods and plantations, the sequence of operations and the reason for these operations. Know some of the dangers to which woods may be exposed, for example, frost, fire and animals.
3. Prepare soil and transplant a young tree.
4. Know how to select, use and care for an axe and the safety rules of axemanship.
5. Know how to fell and trim out a tree.

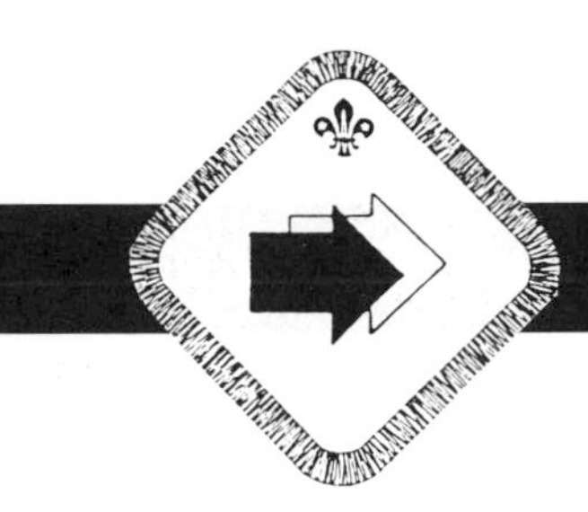

Guide

Service

1. Show (wherever reasonable in a practical way) that you know the locality surrounding your home and Headquarters, up to 2 kilometres radius in boroughs and urban districts and up to 3 kilometres radius in rural districts.

Either:

2. Know the location of the following:
   (a) Doctors, veterinary surgeons, dentists, hospitals and ambulance station.
   (b) Fire station, police station, garages and public telephones.
   (c) Bus stops, railway station(s) and routes of the buses and trains to surrounding areas.
   (d) Local Scout Headquarters, public parks, theatres, cinemas, churches, museums, barracks, public conveniences, and any building or place of local interest.
   (e) Homes of your District Commissioner, Scout Leader, Group Scout Leader and the Scouts in your Patrol.

Or:

For the Metropolitan Police Area the following alternative to requirements 2(a), (b), (c) and (d) is permitted at the discretion of the District Commissioner:

Have a sound general knowledge of which parts of the country are served by the main-line railways and how to reach the principal London railway terminals, the main motor coach stations, the air terminals, and twelve places of national importance (for example The Tower, Zoo and so on) from your Headquarters or home.

3. Show that you understand how to use a map of the district and use it to point out at least six examples in requirement 2. You should guide the examiner by the quickest route to any place covered by the above.
4. Give directions for a person travelling by public transport, cycle or car to a camp site approximately eight kilometres away.

Note:

The Patrol Leaders' Council after consultation with the examiner may, at their discretion, vary the area described in requirement 1 to exclude undesirable neighbourhoods, parks or other open spaces, and include an equivalent area.

Elementary Helmsman

Interest

Qualify for the Royal Yachting Association's Young Sailor Scheme Start Sailing (Stage 1) Award or the National Schools Sailing Association Bronze Award.

In brief summary the Start Sailing (Stage 1) Award includes a practical section including rigging, getting under way, steering and turning, capsize drill and an onshore knowledge section including what to wear, parts of a boat and how to call for assistance.

Notes:

(i) A Scout who gains a similar RYA qualification at an equivalent level qualifies automatically for requirement one of this badge.

(ii) Details of these Awards are available from the Activities office at Gilwell Park or the R.Y.A. at R.Y.A. House, Romsey Road, Eastleigh, Hants SO5 4YA.

Helmsman

Pursuit

Qualify for the Royal Yachting Association's Young Sailor Scheme Start Sailing (Stage 3) Award or the National School Sailing Association Gold Award.

In brief summary the Start Sailing (Stage 3) Award includes rigging in the wind, sailing backwards, capsize and righting procedures, sailing on all points and a knowledge section.

Notes:

(i) A Scout who gains a similar RYA qualification at an equivalent level qualifies automatically for this badge.

(ii) Details of these Awards are available from the Activities office at Gilwell Park or the R.Y.A. at R.Y.A. House, Romsey Road, Eastleigh, Hants SO5 4YA.

Race Helmsman

Pursuit

1. Pass, or have passed, the Helmsman badge. Have a knowledge of the steering and sailing rules, local rules, distress, storm, fog and danger signals.
2. Have a good working knowledge of the yacht racing rules of the International Yacht Racing Union and have a knowledge of the Portsmouth Yardstick Handicapping System.
3. Show by demonstration afloat that you are a proficient helmsman. The demonstration is to include:

   (a) Sailing the boat in any direction on all points of sailing - tack, gybe, reach and run.

   (b) Two race starts by a five-minute gun.

   (c) Efficient mark rounding.

   (d) Hoisting a spinnaker when sailing off the wind if the boat is so equipped.
4. Have some knowledge of modern standing and running rigging, sails and equipment and be able to recognise at least three different classes of modern racing craft.
5. Be able to discuss elementary tactics in relation to racing under sail with particular reference to:

   (a) 'searoom'
   (b) 'establishing on overlap'
   (c) 'giving way'
   (d) 'calling for water'
   (e) 'the use of the centreboard/ dagger board'
   (f) 'spinnakers'

   and show that you understand the general organisation associated with events, including preparatory starting, recall and special signals.
6. Give a reasonable performance as helmsman in a series of three races against young people of your own age. Each race to be between at least three boats and the course in each event to be triangular and over a distance of approximately 2.5 kilometres.

Notes:

(i) The candidate will be judged on general performance rather than on the results of the races. The races may be specially staged or be part of the programme of a Scout Regatta.

(ii) Holders of the R.Y.A. Young Sailors Red Badge qualify automatically for this badge.

Hiker

Collective Achievement

1. Working as a group of at least four and not more than seven Scouts, carry out three hikes as follows:
   (i) a day hike of 12-16km
   (ii) two hikes of 26-32km both of which must include an overnight stop, one of which must be in unfamiliar country.
2. Before undertaking each hike, the group must provide a detailed route card showing estimated times of arrival, map references, route to be followed, bad weather alternatives, camp sites, and so on.
3. Each member of the group must also show that he/she knows the intended route and have a knowledge of simple map reading, the use of a compass, first aid and emergency procedures.
4. After each hike the group must give a verbal report. For at least one of the overnight hikes, the group must make a presentation which may be in the form of a tape recording, log book or photographic record.

Notes:

(i) Reference should be made to Policy, Organisation and Rules.

(ii) Expeditions by canoe, horseback or cycle of similar duration may be acceptable, provided at least one overnight hike on foot is carried out. Cycle helmets should be worn at all times during cycling activities.

(iii) Alternative activities may be carried out as agreed by the Patrol Leaders' Council.

Hillwalker

Interest

1. Keep a log which shows that you have undertaken at least five trips in Moors, Hills and Mountains (as defined in *Policy, Organisation and Rules*) as a member of a properly led group.
2. Help prepare the route cards for the trips, using map and compass, and keep a log of the trips including the route cards, sketch maps and comments on the areas visited. One trip, properly led, should be of two days duration with either a one night camp, bivouac or in a mountain bothy.
3. Show a knowledge of your equipment including:
   (a) What you would wear
   (b) What you would carry in a day rucsac
4. Gain an awareness of the preservation of the natural environment, for example, erosion, wildlife habitat and so on.
5. Have knowledge of the publication *Safety on Mountains (British Mountaineering Council).*

Note:

Reference should be made to Policy, Organisation and Rules and to authorisation rules.

Hobbies and Interest

Interest

1. *Either:*

   Be actively involved with a hobby or interest of your choice not covered by other Proficiency badges and keep a record of your involvement over a period of at least six months.

   Or:

   Make a collection or study of objects over at least six months (for example stamps, metal badges, teaspoons or bookmarks).
2. Demonstrate your knowledge and interest in the subject by discussing the reason for your choice with the examiner.

Note:

For Scouts whose needs are not dealt with in the above, alternative requirements may be adopted as agreed by the Patrol Leaders' Council.

Horseman

Interest

1. Have a firm seat independent of the reins and show that you are able to apply simple aids correctly.
2. Know about the care and working of a pony or horse off grass.
3. Show that you are able to be in control of a pony or horse on the road and in the countryside. Have a proper regard for road sense, safety and courtesy and for country lore.

Note:

A Scout who has qualified for Standard C of The Pony Club qualifies automatically for this badge.

Information Technology

Pursuit

To gain the badge you must pass all the requirements in one of the following alternatives:

A 1. Describe a typical computer system, explaining input, output, memory and storage devices.

2. Use a computer to produce two of the following:
   - (a) Troop newsletter.
   - (b) Troop records.
   - (c) Subscriptions and expenses table.
   - (d) Award progress chart.
   - (e) Map showing local facilities and places of interest.
   - (f) Training presentation.

3. Describe the advantages of computer systems compared to manual systems in two of the following areas:
   - (a) Letter writing.
   - (b) Graphic art, design or drawing.
   - (c) Accounts.
   - (d) Library records.
   - (e) Newspaper layout.
   - (f) Passing messages.
   - (g) News and weather information.
   - (h) Travel and holiday bookings.

4. Explain to the examiner, showing examples, how microprocessors have added to the facilities of everyday devices used in the home or for leisure.

5. (a) Discuss with the examiner and demonstrate an understanding of the laws which concern copying of software, access to computer systems and storage of personal information.
   (b) Discuss with the examiner good and bad practices in the use of computer equipment.

Note:

Information to assist you with this section is available from Headquarters.

B 1. Explain the various types of information systems available and how these can be accessed. For example, Telecom Gold, Prestel, bulletin boards.

2. Explain how a message may be sent on one of the above systems.

3. Explain the legal aspects of accessing other computer systems.

4. Demonstrate one of the following:
   - (a) Make a connection to an on-line database and show the services available and explain how they are used.
   - (b) Use a teletext system to access at least five areas of information including sport, news and weather services. Discuss with the examiner the benefits and limitations of the teletext service.
   - (c) With the help of a radio amateur connect a computer to an amateur radio station and access information from a remote system. Explain in simple terms how the connection is made.

continued overleaf . . .

5. Describe the function of the following:
   Modem;
   RS232/Serial interface;
   Centronics/parallel interface.
6. (a) Discuss with the examiner and demonstrate an understanding of the laws which concern copying of software and storage of personal information.
   (b) Discuss with the examiner good and bad practices in the use of computer equipment.

Notes:

Information to assist you with this section is available from Headquarters.

C 1. (a) Show a working knowledge of a computer language and demonstrate its use by writing a program on a subject agreed with the examiner.
   (b) Run this program using a suitable computer system and show the importance of ease of use and the provision of menus and on-screen help built into the program.
   (c) Explain to the examiner the construction and layout of your program with particular emphasis on structure, presentation and documentation.

2. *Either:*

   Write a flow chart of a routine which you perform daily and a flow chart to show the operation of the program in 1. above.

   Or:

   Draw a block diagram of a typical personal computer showing the component parts such as input, output, memory and storage devices. Briefly explain their function to the examiner.
3. Describe four types of data storage device.
4. Describe six uses of microprocessors, computers or computerised systems.These should include applications in the home, office or industry.
5. (a) Discuss with the examiner and demonstrate an understanding of the laws which concern copying of software, access to computer systems and storage of personal information.
   (b) Discuss with the examiner good and bad practices in the use of computer equipment.

Notes:

Information to assist you with this section is available from Headquarters.

Interpreter

Service

To gain the badge you must complete all the requirements in one of the following alternatives:

A Complete the following in any language other than your own.

1. Carry on a simple conversation for approximately ten minutes.
2. Write a letter of approximately 150 words dealing with a Scout topic.
3. After a few minutes for study, give an approximate translation of a paragraph from a newspaper or periodical.
4. Assist as interpreter for a foreign visitor.
5. *Either:*

   Write letters for a Scout Group, school or similar body, for example helping with the arrangements for a foreign visit or exchange.

   Or:

   Correspond regularly for not less than one year with a Scout or person of Scout age of another country.

B Complete the following requirements in a recognised sign language such as Makaton or BSL.

1. Carry out a simple conversation for approximately ten minutes.
2. Describe a Scouting experience to another person.
3. Act as a translator for a short conversation between a sign language user and someone with no sign language experience.
4. Invite a sign language user to talk to your Troop about the experience of having hearing or speech impediments, or both. Act as translator for them during their visit.

Librarian

Interest

1. *Either:*

   Supply the examiner with a list of at least twelve books which you have read in the previous twelve months. Explain why you read them, what you thought of them and answer questions about their contents.

   The list should include both fiction and non-fiction, with not more than three books by any one author, and should exclude school text books.

   Or:

   Supply the examiner with a short bibliography dealing with a subject in which you are specially interested. Explain your choice of books to the examiner and answer questions about their contents.

2. Demonstrate a knowledge of the care of books.

3. Show that you know how to use a library catalogue. This could include the subject index or on-line computer catalogues. Explain how fiction and non-fiction books are arranged on the shelves and why they are treated differently.

4. Know what is meant by a reference book. What sort of information could you obtain from the following types of books: dictionaries, timetables, almanacs, gazettes, Who's Who and so on.

Lifesaver

Service

1. Hold the Swimmer badge and understand and explain how you would effect a rescue using the following methods: reach, throw, wade and row.
2. Hold the Lifesaving 3 Award of the Royal Life Saving Society U.K.
3. Show methods of rescue used in the case of ice-breaking, house fire, gas poisoning, car accident and contact with live electric wire.

Notes:

(i) In brief summary the Life Saving 3 Award includes dealing with a distressed casualty, rescuing an unconscious casualty, recovering a casualty from a depth and a knowledge section.

(ii) Holders of the BCU Canoeing Safety Test qualify for requirement 2 of this badge.

Local Heritage

Pursuit

To gain the badge you must pass the requirements in one of the following alternatives:

A Over a period of at least three months, or thirty hours, with others be involved in a project which helps preserve an aspect of your local heritage (for example steam railway, archaeological site, historic monument or museum).

B Over a period of at least three months be involved with a group that keeps alive traditional entertainment and take part in at least one public performance (for example clog dancing, folk singing, musical group or band).

C With others learn about an aspect of your local heritage or history and mount a display, exhibition or presentation of your work. This could be a local custom or craft, the history of a local building or the life of a famous person from history with connections to your local area.

Master-at-Arms

Pursuit

1. Demonstrate proficiency in an armed activity such as fencing, rifle shooting or archery.
2. Know the safety rules associated with your chosen activity and demonstrate their use.
3. Have attended regular training sessions in the selected activity for a period of not less than three months and demonstrate an improvement in your ability over that period.
4. Take part in the selected activity in a properly supervised contest and discuss your performance with the examiner.

Mechanic

Pursuit

To gain the badge you must pass all the requirements in one of the following alternatives:

A 1. Know the principles of operation of an internal combustion engine and understand the function of the clutch, gearbox and rear axle differential of a motor car.

2. Remove, clean and check the gap of a sparking plug.

3. Check and top up the level of oil in a motor car engine. Explain the purpose of the oil and oil filter and the procedure for changing them.

4. Remove and replace a road wheel. Know the precautions to observe, check tyre pressures and depth of tread. Understand the reasons why cross and radial ply tyres should not be mixed on the same axle.

B 1. Show by demonstration that when operating the engine of a power craft you can respond quickly to orders given by the coxswain.

2. *Either:*

(a) Be able to discuss the principles and performance of several types of motor boat engines (other than two-stroke) and show a knowledge of the special care and maintenance needed by a type of small marine internal combustion engine familiar to you (other than two-stroke).

Or:

(b) Have a working knowledge of small motor boat four-stroke engines generally and show a knowledge of the special servicing required by a small marine diesel unit.

Or:

(c) With minimum assistance dismantle, thoroughly service and re-assemble an outboard engine and demonstrate proper fitting to the transom of a boat. Be able to explain how to detect minor faults in starting and running whilst afloat.

3. *Either:*

(a) As driver/mechanic member of a power boat's crew, assist in the preparation of the boat for a voyage by checking the engine for possible minor faults, checking the fuel supply and pump, and mustering the fire-fighting equipment. In response to orders operate the engine whilst getting underway from the quay. Whilst afloat, demonstrate how to deal with minor running defects in compression, ignition, electrics, filters, intake and outlet and in over-oiling. Operate the engine to bring the craft alongside the quay and shut-down. Lay out a kedge anchor.

continued overleaf . . .

(b) Re-man the boat in response to a 'distress call' and under orders, start and operate the engine whilst proceeding to and manoeuvring alongside a 'stranded craft'. This part of the test is to include operation of all gears in a confined area of water and a return journey to base, coming alongside with the tide (or current). Know how to leave the engine in a proper manner and how to drain the engine in an emergency.

Or:

(a) Act as mechanic on at least one short cruise or expedition and be responsible for the running of the engine throughout the cruise.

(b) Thoroughly check and service the engine of a motor boat in preparation for a cruise or expedition to include the provision of fuel and safe storage, an adequate tool kit and effective fire fighting appliances. Accompany the expedition either as the mechanic or assistant mechanic and be responsible (or jointly responsible) for the operation, care and maintenance of the engine throughout.

C 1. Understand the basic principles of, and be able to point out the component parts of *either:*

(a) an aircraft piston engine;

Or:

(b) an aircraft gas turbine engine.

2. Understand the basic principles of flight of a fixed wing aircraft.

3. Know and be able to demonstrate Aircraft Marshalling signals used by day and night.

4. Demonstrate your ability to carry out four of the following:

(a) Replenish a light aircraft fuel and oil system.

(b) Rig and de-rig a glider.

(c) Picket a light aircraft.

(d) Change a set of plugs on a light aircraft engine.

(e) Inspect aircraft main and tail (or nose) wheel tyres for serviceability.

(f) Repair a small tear in the fabric surface of a light aircraft or glider.

(g) The pre-use inspection of a parachute and how to put it on and take it off.

(h) Check the control system of a light aircraft or glider for correct sense of movement.

D 1. Know the principles of operation of a two-stroke or four-stroke internal combustion engine and understand the function of the clutch, gearbox, carburettor and transmission of a motor cycle.

2. Remove, clean and check the gap of a sparking plug.

3. Clean and top up a motor cycle battery. Understand the basic electrical circuit of a motor cycle including the frame earth concept. Be able to identify and change a fuse.

4. Check and top up the level of the engine oil.

5. Explain how to adjust the tension of the final drive chain.

6. Describe the procedure for removing and replacing both road wheels.

7. Check the tyre pressure and depth of tread.

Meteorologist

Pursuit

1. Keep a daily record of the weather from your own observations for at least one month to include at least four of the following:
   Wind force and direction;
   Cloud type and amount;
   Weather - using Beaufort scale;
   Temperature;
   Pressure;
   Rainfall amount.
2. Understand the working principles of the following instruments and construct a simple version of one of them:
   Thermometer;
   Barometer;
   Sunshine recorder;
   Anemometer;
   Rain gauge.
3. Understand at least three different ways in which clouds are formed.
4. Know the typical weather produced in your own area by 'warm' and 'cold' air masses in summer and winter, noting the different effects of land and sea tracks. Understand the weather associated with a change of air mass at 'fronts'.
5. Know how synoptic weather maps are produced and be able to understand a simple map, with fronts and isobars, similar to those shown on television and printed in some newspapers. Relate your observations in requirement 1 to these maps.
6. Understand the effects of temperature, wind and water on the human body in cases of hypothermia and exhaustion.

Model Maker

Pursuit

To gain this badge you must complete all the requirements in one of the following alternatives:

A 1. Construct a model aeroplane (the use of a kit is permitted) which, when flown, meets one of the following minimum flight performances:

Glider (hand launched) - 25 seconds.

Glider (tow launched with 50 metres maximum line length) - 45 seconds.

Rubber-powered - 30 seconds.

Engine-powered - (15 seconds maximum motor run) - 45 seconds.

Control line: demonstrate your model by making a smooth take off, three laps level flight at approximately 2 metres and climb and dive with a smooth landing.

2. Have a knowledge of the basic principles of flight, including the three axes and their effect on stability and control.

B 1. Build an electric or engine-powered model boat or yacht, not less than 45cm in length (kits permitted) and show it to be capable of maintaining a straight course of not less than 25 metres.

2. Give a clear explanation of Archimedes' Principles.

C 1. *Either:*

Build an electric slot car racer (not from a kit, though a commercial body and other parts may be used) and drive it a minimum distance of 122 metres on any track without stopping or leaving the slot more than four times.

Or:

Build a free running car of any type (kits permitted) and demonstrate that it will run for at least 18 metres. Airscrew drive is allowed.

2. Know how track and wheelbase are measured and sketch and explain Ackerman steering.

D 1. Build a coach or wagon and demonstrate that it runs satisfactorily behind a locomotive.

2. Build a scenic model, such as a station, farmhouse and so on, (kits allowed) to scale for a layout.

3. Draw an electric circuit for a simple track layout.

4. Detail the safety precautions to be taken when assembling such a layout.

Note:

Headquarters will provide on request, requirements for this badge for a Scout whose needs are not dealt with in the above.

Mountaineer

Pursuit

1. Hold the Hillwalker badge.
2. Be fully conversant with the contents of the publication *Safety on Mountains (British Mountaineering Council).*
3. Demonstrate that you have a knowledge of a mountain area covering at least 50 sq km by producing journey notes and log books of journeys in the area. These notes must show:
   (a) That you are personally acquainted with principal routes for summits and the approximate time it would take to complete various day journeys in the area.
   (b) That you are acquainted with places of interest in the area, such as nature conservancy, water conservancy, quarrying or mining and have some knowledge of them.
   (c) That you know the nearest telephones, Doctors, inns and places of refreshment and shelter in the area.
4. Plan a route by completing all the information requested on the Scout Route Plan for a day journey in the area from a 1:50 000 scale or 1:25 000 Ordnance Survey map, working out six figure grid references as required.
5. Using a map out of doors, demonstrate your ability to identify open mountainous country. All of the features seen on the land should be identified on the map and vice versa.
6. Discuss local weather conditions and demonstrate your ability to understand weather forecasts such as appear in the daily press and television.
7. Show a knowledge of your equipment including:
   (a) What you would wear.
   (b) What you would carry in a day rucsac.
8. Complete all the information requested on the Scout Emergency Card and outline in detail the procedure in the event of an accident including:
   (a) Care and treatment of the patient and what can be best done by the person remaining with an injured person.
   (b) How, and with what, to give a distress signal.
   (c) The procedure for an emergency bivouac.
9. Demonstrate your knowledge of hypothermia including:
   (a) Causes of hypothermia and exhaustion.
   (b) How to avoid hypothermia and exhaustion.
   (c) Recognise symptoms in a person suffering from hypothermia and exhaustion.
   (d) How to deal with a person suffering from hypothermia and exhaustion (on a mountain and at base).

continued overleaf . . .

10. Discuss the need to conserve the mountain environment and the possible damage caused by those walking and climbing in the mountains.

Notes:

(i) It is recommended that reference be made to the book Mountaincraft and Leadership *by Eric Langmuir.*

(ii) Route plans and emergency cards are available from the Resource Centre at Gilwell Park.

Musician

Interest

To gain this badge you must complete all the requirements in one of the following alternatives:

A 1. Sing a solo with accompaniment or take part in a part song.

2. Read at sight three songs.
3. Know some basic principles and fundamentals of music as appropriate to your chosen form of singing.
4. Discuss with the examiner some appropriate recent performances you have heard at concerts, on radio or television, or from a recording.

B 1. *Either:*

(a) Sing unaccompanied two different types of folk song - for example spiritual and sea shanty, mountain song and lullaby.

Or:

(b) Sing, with your own accompaniment (banjo, guitar, mandolin, and so on), two different types of folk song.

Or:

(c) Play two different types of folk music on a banjo, guitar, mandolin, concertina, harmonica or other folk instrument.

2. Know some basic principles and fundamentals of music, such as tuning your own instrument, keys, chords and bass notes.
3. Discuss with the examiner some of the types of folk music and performers or artists which you enjoy. You must be prepared to give reasons for your choice.

C For musical instruments not covered elsewhere in this badge:

1. Play two solos, one of your own choice and the other at sight, on any recognised musical instrument other than a percussion instrument.
2. *Either*

Produce a concerted item with others, in which you must play the instrument used in requirement 1.

Or:

Play another solo of different type and speed than those played in requirement 1.

3. Know some basic principles and fundamentals of music as appropriate to your chosen instrument.
4. Discuss with the examiner some appropriate recent performances you have heard at concerts, on radio or TV, or from a recording.

continued overleaf . . .

D 1. Show that you can tune your pipes properly.

2. Play two bagpipe marches in 2/4 time.
3. Play two bagpipe marches in 6/8 time.
4. Play a slow march or slow air.
5. Play a march, strathspey and reel. (The march may be one of those played in requirement 2.)

Note:

(i) All tunes to be of your own choice.

(ii) When Northumbrian or Irish pipes are used, alternatives may be used at the examiner's discretion.

E As a Percussion Drummer:

1. Be a member of a musical group, either at school, in your Scout Group, or other organisation.
2. Take part in a stage presentation.
3. Perform routine maintenance on your instrument.
4. Perform basic drum rudiments.
5. Play a good class roll in the following form:

   3 paces roll;

   5 paces roll;

   7 paces roll.
6. Take part satisfactorily in six different pieces of music.

F 1. Be a member of a Band in which you have served for a minimum of six months, either at school, in your Scout Group, Scout District or other organisation and provide proof of regular attendance.

2. If a member of a uniformed marching Band:
   (a) Present yourself for examination in full and correct Bandsman's uniform and demonstrate an understanding of why a Bandsman's turnout should be smart and correct.
   (b) Demonstrate your proficiency in basic drill movements including marking time, turns, wheels, counter-marching and carrying of instruments, in both quick time and slow time.
3. Present your instrument and accessories for inspection and demonstrate your ability to perform routine maintenance and, where applicable, tuning of your instrument.
4. Take part satisfactorily in six different marches, playing one of the undermentioned instruments:

   SNARE DRUM

   (a) Beat in 2/4, 3/4 and 6/8 time.
   (b) Play 'off beats' in 2/4, 3/4 and 6/8 time.
   (c) Play a proficient closed roll in the following forms:
      (i) 3 pace roll;
      (ii) 5 pace roll;
      (iii) 7 pace roll.
   (d) Demonstrate dynamics technique.
   (e) Show a good proficiency of stick drill.
   (f) March over a distance of at least 50 metres, beating a strict quick march tempo.
   (g) March over a distance of at least 50 metres, beating a strict slow march tempo.
   (h) Play a drum solo of your choice.

BUGLES/TRUMPETS/VALVED BRASS COMBINATION/ WOODWIND/REED INSTRUMENTS

(a) Play two solos of your own choice.

(b) Demonstrate an understanding of the terms attack, tone and dynamics.

(c) Perform tongued and slurred notes.

(d) (i) Bugle - play as a solo 'Sunset' and 'Last Post'.

(ii) Valved instruments - play as a solo 'The National Anthem'.

MALLETS

(a) Play 2 solos of your own choice.

(b) Demonstrate the correct hand to hand execution techniques.

(c) Demonstrate the use of simple chords.

(d) Demonstrate 2/4, 3/4 and 4/4 time.

(e) Demonstrate an open roll in 3/4 time.

CYMBALS

(a) Show proficient cymbal drill when playing at the halt and on the march with simple 'flourishing'.

(b) Demonstrate 'off beat' technique in 2/4, 3/4 and 4/4 time.

(c) March over adistance of at least 50 metres, beating a strict quick march tempo.

(d) March over a distance of at least 50 metres, beating a strict slow march tempo.

TENOR/MULTI-TOMS/ BASS DRUM

(a) Show proficient stick drill and flourishing whilst beating at the halt and on the march.

(b) Demonstrate 2/4, 3/4 and 6/8 time.

(c) Tenors and Multi-toms to demonstrate off beats in 2/4, 3/4 and 6/8 time.

(d) March over a distance of at least 50 metres, beating a strict quick march temo.

(e) March over a distance of at least 50 metres, beating a strict slow march tempo.

FIFES

(a) Play a march in 2/4 time.

(b) Play a march in 6/8 time.

(c) Play a slow march.

(d) Play as a solo 'The National Anthem'.

Notes:

These marches to be played whilst actually marching and, if necessary, may be accompanied by other instruments to complete harmonies.

continued overleaf . . .

DRUM MAJOR/FIELD COMMANDER

(a) Explain your understanding of a Drum Major/Field Commander's control of the band/corps and the importance of:

(i) clear signals and words of command;

(ii) the ability to make on the spot decisions.

(b) Command your band to fall in correctly and dress off.

DRUM MAJOR

(i) Demonstrate, whilst on the march, signals for left/right wheel, countermarch, mark time, short step, advance, stop playing, recommence playing and halt.

(ii) Demonstrate ability to march correctly in quick and slow time whilst carrying a mace and the returning of a salute on the march and at a halt.

(iii) Demonstrate simple showmanship with the mace.

FIELD COMMANDER

(c) (i) Demonstrate and have an understanding of basic conducting techniques.

(ii) Control band whilst playing, at the halt, a march in strict tempo and music in a display routine.

(d) Explain the corrective measures faced with the following four possible emergencies that could arise in an otherwise routine parade or display.

(i) animals;

(ii) traffic;

(iii) other bands;

(iv) emergency vehicles.

My Faith

Interest

You may work for this Badge either by yourself or with other Scouts.

Make an action plan which will help you to find out about your religious community and be more involved in its life.

When you have carried out your action plan, meet with the Patrol Leaders' Council and tell them what you have done.

The action plan will list four definite activities which you should undertake over a period of not less than three months.

It may help you in your planning if you speak with your Scout Leader, someone at home, or someone at your place of worship.

Once you have decided on your plan, and the period of time for it, the plan should be agreed with your Patrol Leaders' Council.

The activities in your plan should include two areas from A and two from B. Examples of each activity are given but they are just that: simply examples. You may well have much better ideas for your action plan.

A KNOWLEDGE AND UNDERSTANDING

1. Find out more about the origin of your religion and present your findings in some suitable way. This could be done, for example, through a series of tape recorded interviews with members of your religious community.
2. Explore the history of your faith. This may be at the local, national, or international level. You could, for example, find out about some important people in the history of your faith or you could visit a place which has religious importance for your faith and find out as much as you can about it.
3. Be able to explain some of the beliefs of your faith. For example, you could discover and explain the meaning of some of the important festivals in your religious community.

B ACTIVE MEMBERSHIP

1. Take an active part in the place of worship of your religion. For example, you could volunteer to take a special part in the services where this is possible.
2. Be active in the life of your religious community. For example, you could take part in the Youth Programme and take a leading role in at least two activities.
3. Be involved with your place of worship in some community work. For example, you might help with visiting the elderly or sick.
4. Find out about a religious community other than your own. You might do this, for example, through a discussion with a Scout in your Troop.

C THE AWARDING OF THE BADGE

The Badge is to be awarded by the Patrol Leaders' Council in consultation with the Scout Leader and a religious leader of your community.

Naturalist

Pursuit

1. Study the natural history (such as plants and animals) during any two of the seasons (spring, summer, autumn or winter) of one of the following:

Either:

(a) a piece of woodland;

(b) a piece of parkland;

(c) a piece of downland;

(d) a piece of moorland;

(e) a piece of sea shore, sand-dune or rocks.

The area studied should be approximately one acre (5,000 square metres or half hectare) in size.

Or:

(f) a length of hedgerow;

(g) a length of roadside verge;

(h) a length of stream, river or canal;

(i) a small pond of not less than 90 metres.

Explain the results of the study to the examiner, using field notes, simple sketches or photographs and sketch maps.

2. Discuss with the examiner how the natural history of the site studied could be affected by man's activities or management, for example replacing deciduous trees with conifers, waste oil discharged by oil tankers at sea, cutting hedges and roadside verges by machine instead of manually.

3. Make a detailed study of any one plant or animal (for example a fern, grass, wild flower, tree or shrub; butterfly, moth or other insect; amphibian, wild animal, bird, fish and so on). Discuss with the examiner the results of your observations and the sources of any information used, for example museums, books and so on.

Navigator

Pursuit

To gain the badge you must pass all the requirements in one of the following alternatives:

A 1. Using 1:50 000 scale Ordnance Survey maps and a 1:10 000 scale orienteering map, with examples set by the examiner:

(a) Show that you understand the meaning of scale, National Grid Reference and true, grid and magnetic north and can recognise conventional map signs.

(b) Interpret contour lines in terms of shape and steepness of terrain and know the local names and meanings of topographical features such as col, ridge, spur, and so on.

(c) Show how to set the map with and without a compass. Be able to use and to give six - figure grid references and demonstrate the use of a Romer measurer to improve accuracy.

(d) Show how to measure distance on the map and how to estimate timings for a particular route.

(e) Show how to find north without the aid of a compass, by day or night.

2. Know how the national system of road numbering works and be familiar with the traffic signs and signals as illustrated in the *Highway Code.*

3. Accompany a motorist or motorcyclist as a passenger and act successfully as a navigator for a total journey of at least 160 kilometres. For a specified section of the journey, covering a distance of 80 kilometres, prepare and use an AA or RAC type strip-route map. The journey should also include navigating with no previous preparation of the route.

4. Complete, accurately, a compass route of at least two kilometres as defined on a map supplied by the examiner. During this exercise show that you can:

(a) Convert grid bearings to magnetic bearings and vice versa.

(b) Use back bearings to check your route.

(c) Pinpoint your position using three cross-bearings.

5. Take part in two properly organised orienteering events and show an improvement in your performance. Demonstrate methods of route selection including aiming off and the four right angles and step counting techniques.

B1. Given a series of three headings and corresponding tracks, work out in each case the type and the amount of drift in degrees and illustrate each case by a simple diagram.

continued overleaf . . .

2. Demonstrate with a compass how an aircraft can be turned on to three successive compass headings.
3. *Either:*

   Draw on a topographical air map a track for an imaginary flight of not less than 80 kilometres and point out the landmarks which would show up on both sides of the track in clear visibility at an altitude of about 600 metres.

   Or:

   Identify on a topographical air map landmarks seen during a flight of about half an hour's duration in clear weather.
4. Illustrate by means of a simple diagram how a fix can be obtained from two position lines. Describe briefly two ways in which bearings can be obtained in an aircraft, thus enabling position lines to be drawn on a chart.
5. (a) Given the true heading and the variation and deviation, work out the compass heading on which the pilot should be flying.

   (b) Given two sets of true, magnetic and compass headings, work out the variation and deviation in each case.
6. Illustrate by simple diagrams latitude and longitude.
7. Draw on a topographical map the track between any two places not less than 100 kilometres apart and measure the exact distance; given the aircraft's air speed as 130 km/h, work out the time of flight from overhead starting point to overhead destination in each of the following conditions:
   (a) With no wind at all.
   (b) With a head wind of 30 km/h.
   (c) With a tail wind of 50 km/h.

C 1. Have a good working knowledge of charts, including the projection, datum and symbols used and the tidal information given.

2. (a) Read a mariner's compass marked in points and degrees and have a knowledge of compasses generally, including variation and deviation.

   (b) Be able to apply variation and deviation to a compass course or bearing to obtain a true reading. Give a true reading to obtain a compass course.

   (c) Understand how compass error can be found from a transit bearing.
3. (a) Understand the theory of how a position may be found from any two position lines.

   (b) Plot a position from any three cross bearings. Understand what is meant by a 'cocked hat' and how to use it safely.

   (c) Plot a position using the 'running fix' method.

   (d) Plot a position using a combination of compass bearings and any one or more of the following:
   Decca or satellite navigation system;
   Vertical sextant angle;
   Horizontal sextant angle;
   Line of soundings;
   Transits.
4. Have a working knowledge of tide tables and tidal stream atlases.
5. Understand the use of the marine log to obtain distance, run and speed.
6. Understand the buoyage system for United Kingdom coastal waters and other methods of marking dangers and channels.

continued overleaf . . .

7. Undertake a coastal voyage of at least six hours acting as navigator. A log must be kept showing the courses steered, distance run, navigation marks passed and weather experienced.During the voyage:

   (a) Plot the estimated position every hour by keeping up the dead reckoning.

   (b) Whenever appropriate, and not less than once per hour, plot an observed position by bearings or other means of obtaining a fix.

Note:

The voyage, which need not have a definite destination, should be planned on the chart beforehand using tidal streams to the best advantage and giving hourly courses to steer for an assumed speed.

Observer

Interest

1. In a Kim's game, remember 24 out of 30 well-assorted articles after one minute's observation. The game is to be performed twice running with different articles and each article is to be adequately described.
2. By hearing alone, recognise eight out of ten simple sounds.
3. Give an accurate report of an incident lasting not less than one minute and involving three persons. This report, verbal or written, must include a full description of one of the persons involved, selected by the examiner.
4. Make six plaster casts of the tracks of birds, animals, car or bicycle. All casts are to be taken unaided and correctly labelled with the date and place of making. At least two should be of wild birds or animals.
5. Follow a trail two kilometers in length containing approximately 40 signs made of natural materials. The route should be over unfamiliar ground. Roads may be crossed but not followed.

Orienteering

Interest

1. Demonstrate a knowledge of the Country Code.
2. Show an understanding of safety procedures, basic first aid, appropriate clothing and equipment required for countryside navigation.
3. Explain the following principles of orienteering:
   (a) Check points.
   (b) Attack points.
   (c) Route planning and the importance of contours.
4. Using a 1:10,000 orienteering map show an ability to set the map and transfer relevant details from a master map.
5. Take part in a competitive orienteering event and complete the course.

Paraglider

Pursuit

1. Know the rules relating to access to airfields as laid down in *Policy, Organisation and Rules.* Understand the factors involved in selecting the launch point on the field.
2. Successfully complete the British Hang-gliding and Paragliding Association's Paragliding Ground Training, including landing rolls and inflation and collapse of canopy by wing-tip holders and paragliders.
3. Carry out the British Hang-gliding and Paragliding Association's Course of Training in controlled descents, and self-released flights up to the standard of 360 degree stable turns.
4. Carry out canopy control practice on the ground and have a basic knowledge of the flight and steering principles of the canopy.
5. Understand and perform the duties of wing-tip holder, look-out and tensiometer reader, and understand the function of the launch marshal.
6. Understand the care, packing and storage of equipment.

Note:

A Scout must not attempt the requirements of this badge until he or she is at least 14 years old.

Photographer

Interest

To gain the badge you must complete all the requirements in one of the following alternatives:

A

1. *Either:*

   Produce 12 photographs, taken by yourself, covering at least two of the subjects from the following:
   portrait;
   still life or similar;
   land or seascape;
   sport or similar action;
   flash-gun;
   time-lapse photography.

   Or:

   Produce six black and white photographs where you have undertaken some part of the processing yourself.

2. Discuss with the examiner the main functions of a camera including shutter speeds, apertures, film speed, depth of field and lens focusing.

3. Discuss the different types of camera on the market and the various accessories used by today's photographer, both to ensure quality of results and to create effects. Explain the difference between camera shake and movement.

4. Describe the process of developing black and white films and prints, including the use of an enlarger.

5. Diagnose faults that occur both at the photographing and printing stages such as over/under exposure and high/low contrast.

6. Demonstrate a knowledge of photography by artificial light by arranging equipment provided by yourself or the examiner for a portrait, still life or similar subject.

B

1. Produce at least two short films, using two of the following categories:
   (a) Documentary;
   (b) Music video;
   (c) Drama;
   (d) Situation comedy;
   (e) Advertisement;
   (f) Training film;
   (g) Environmental;
   (h) Community;
   (i) Current affairs.

For each of these you should produce a story board and script. The film can be either edited 'in camera' or by using simple editing equipment.

2. (a) Understand the main features and functions of a video camera including zoom, focus, aperture, shutter speed, white balance and common domestic tape formats.

   (b) Discuss with the examiner problems that may be encountered when using automatic settings and how these problems may be overcome.

3. Show an understanding of the following:

   (a) Camera techniques such as panning, zooming, the use of close-ups, long shots and the use of additional lighting and so on.

   (b) Production techniques such as editing, how to avoid jumpy cuts, maintaining continuity and so on.

4. Demonstrate that you know how to care for a video camera and accessories such as tapes, batteries, microphones and lights.

Note:

Section B1. can be completed as a small group with each person taking a different responsibility, for example camera operator, director, actor. Each separate film should use different people in different roles.

Pioneer

Collective Achievement

1. Demonstrate and know the uses of the following knots and lashings: sheet bend, clove hitch, round turn and two half hitches, bowline, timber hitch, sheepshank, square and sheer lashings.
2. Demonstrate the following:
   (a) West Country or simple whipping;
   (b) The correct way to coil a rope;
   (c) The use of simple blocks and tackle;
   (d) The use of levers to extract or move heavy weights;
   (e) An understanding of the need for supervision and safety in pioneering projects.
3. As a member of a group of three to six Scouts, complete the following:
   (a) Take part in an indoor pioneering project;
   (b) Take part in building a pioneering model;
   (c) Take part in constructing an outdoor pioneering project.

Note:
Alternative activities may be undertaken as agreed by the Patrol Leaders' Council.

Advanced Pioneer

Collective Achievement

1. Pass or have passed the Pioneer badge.
2. Demonstrate, and know the uses of, the following knots and lashings:
   (a) Harvesters' hitch;
   (b) Double sheetbend;
   (c) Fisherman's knot;
   (d) Rolling hitch;
   (e) Figure of eight lashing;
   (f) Diagonal lashing.
3. Demonstrate the following:
   (a) Sailmakers' whipping;
   (b) Eye and back splices;
   (c) Anchorage for firm and soft ground.
4. Have a knowledge of the following:
   (a) The construction of man-made and natural fibre ropes and their breaking strains.
   (b) *The Aerial Runway Code.*
   (c) How to store and maintain pioneering equipment.
5. As a member of a group of three to six Scouts design and build two projects as agreed with the examiner beforehand.

Note:
Alternative activities may be undertaken as agreed by the Patrol Leaders' Council after consultation with the badge examiner.

Power Coxswain

Pursuit

A Powerboats

1. Have a detailed knowledge of the steering and sailing rules for power and sailing vessels and show by demonstration, using diagrams or models, that you have a practical knowledge of local waters, including:
   (a) Tides and/or currents.
   (b) Local hazards, sandbars, shallows, rocks, underwater obstructions and any dangerous features such as weirs.
   (c) Lights, daymarks and buoyage in relation to local water traffic, including fishing craft and fishing grounds.
   (d) Alteration of course and turning signals.
2. Know the safety precautions necessary in power craft, including the proper use of fire-fighting appliances and 'man overboard' drill.
3. Have a knowledge of the elementary principles of the motor boat engine and by demonstration afloat show:
   (a) That you can start the engine, operate the gears and understand the effect of transverse thrust with a single screw.
   (b) That you can turn circles using reverse gear, control the boat in confined waters and stop the engine when going slow ahead.
   (c) That you can recognise the minor faults in an engine.
4. Take charge of a small crew and prepare the boat for service, to include the provision of all equipment. Supervise checking the engine, fuel and pump, and then:
   (a) Show that you can operate the correct towing procedure, including disposition of crew, and that you are familiar with the use of the kedge anchor in an emergency.
   (b) With minimum assistance, cast off with the tide (or current) ahead using the spring method. Steer a compass course (as set by the examiner) and anchor correctly. Recover the ground tackle, get under way and return alongside against the tide (or current) without using reverse gear. Moor with spring and headrope.
   (c) Respond to a 'distress' signal, take charge of the crew, cast off with the tide (or current) astern, using the spring and headrope method and proceed to a 'stranded craft' (aground in confined waters). Approach across the tide (or current) and take aboard a 'survivor'; manoeuvre clear, using reverse gear, and proceed to pick up a 'body' (not an actual person) from the water. Bring your boat alongside with tide (or current), using reverse gear, giving appropriate orders to crew, and make fast. Supervise preparations necessary to disembark the 'casualty'.

continued overleaf . . .

Notes:

(i) The conditions described are designed for the use of inboard power craft and this type of craft should be used if practicable.

(ii) For the use of outboard motor craft the tests should be modified accordingly, for example:

2. Include use of engine safety cut-out (kill cord).

3. (a) Include some 'additional practical knowledge in care and maintenance of outboard engine' and 'mixture of fuel and lubricant'.

3. (b) Modify accordingly.

4. (c) Substitute 'veer down on wreck using anchor'.

(iii) Holders of the R.Y.A. National Powerboat Certificate 2 qualify automatically for parts 1, 2 and 3 of this badge.

B Narrowboats

1. Have a detailed knowledge of the steering of a narrowboat on canals and have a knowledge of a canal including:
   (a) Suitable places to moor and wind;
   (b) Locks, bridges and local hazards;
   (c) Water points, sanitary stations;
   (d) Shops and telephones.
2. Know the safety precautions necessary in narrowboats including:
   (a) Fire-fighting appliances;
   (b) 'Man overboard' drill;
   (c) Locks;
   (d) Tunnels.
3. Have a knowledge of the elementary principles of a marine engine and by demonstration afloat show:
   (a) That you can start and stop the engine, operate the gears and understand the effect of transverse thrust with a single screw.
   (b) That you can turn the boat in a winding hole and control the boat in confined waters.
   (c) That you can recognise fouling of the screw due to weed or rubbish and know how to clear it with special emphasis on immobilising the engine.
   (d) Demonstrate how to use the stern gland screw.
4. Take charge of the boat under qualified supervision and complete the following manoeuvres:
   (a) Prepare the boat for service and, with the help of a crew, cast off and leave your moorings.
   (b) With the help of a crew take the boat through a lock.
   (c) Show that you can steer the boat past moored boats, past a boat moving towards you and through a bridge hole, and show that you can moor the boat.
   (d) Whilst moving forward, stop and reverse the boat to an object dropped in the water. Be aware of the dangers to a person in the water from a moving screw.

Public Relations

Pursuit

1. Give a five minute verbal presentation about Scouting using some visual aids.
2. Obtain some media coverage for a Scouting event, expedition or activity. This can be done by preparing a press release, taking a photograph, producing a publication or writing a short article for the Group, District or County newsletter, Parish magazine or similar.
3. Assist the Group/District/County with a promotional event.
4. Complete two of the following:
   (a) Produce at least four editions of a newsletter for your Patrol or Troop.
   (b) Create a simple display or exhibition to show Cub Scouts the fun of being a Scout or for use at an open evening for parents.
   (c) Arrange a visit for a Patrol to the local newspaper or radio or television station (including hospital radio).
   (d) Prepare and carry out a simple survey to determine the image of Scouting locally amongst your friends. Report the findings to your Scout Leader and Patrol Leaders' Council.

Pulling

Collective Achievement

Theory

1. Have a basic knowledge of boat parts and their uses including:
   (a) Rudder;
   (b) Stretcher;
   (c) Painter;
   (d) Pintle and gudgeon;
   (e) Transom;
   (f) Fairlead;
   (g) Tiller;
   (h) Thwart;
   (i) Gunwale;
   (j) Oars;
   (k) Crutches;
   (l) Skulling notch;
   (m) Rowlocks;
   (n) Thole pins.
2. Know the rules of the road, including steering and sailing rules.
3. Know about safety afloat including lifejackets, buoyancy aids and different health hazards (including Weil's disease).
4. Have an understanding of the causes and treatment of hypothermia and blisters.
5. Understand the principles of holding station and coming up to a buoy.

Practical

1. Be able to swim 50 metres in ordinary clothes and keep afloat for five minutes.
2. Demonstrate an ability to tie the following bends and hitches and know their uses.
   (a) Sheetbend;
   (b) Bowline;
   (c) Double sheetbend;
   (d) Fisherman's bend;
   (e) Clovehitch;
   (f) Round turn and two half hitches;
   (g) Reef knot.
3. Demonstrate crewing a boat under oars and handling of boats ashore including:
   (a) Entering and leaving the boat properly;
   (b) Moving around it safely;
   (c) Pulling using the correct techniques;
   (d) Stowing oars;
   (e) Coming alongside;
   (f) Making boat fast;
   (g) After use;
   (h) Boat orders;
   (i) Removing rowlocks;
   (j) Securing to trolley.
4. Crew in a gig (or similar craft) and show an understanding of at least ten pulling orders including those given in emergencies.

Quartermaster

Service

To gain the badge you must complete all the requirements in one of the following alternatives.

A 1. Have assisted the Group or Troop Quartermaster effectively for a period of six months.

2. Understand and be prepared to demonstrate:
   (a) The care of ropes, for example whipping, splicing, hanking, coiling, inspection and storing.
   (b) The safe handling and storage of fuels.
   (c) The care of cooking equipment, for example repairing, cleaning, inspection and storing.
3. Understand and demonstrate how to keep simple and efficient records, including issue and returns of Group or Troop equipment.
4. Understand and be prepared to demonstrate the storage of a Section's equipment.
5. Understand the care and storage of group visual aid equipment.
6. Understand how to deal practically with depreciation of all equipment.
7. Understand that general tidiness is the secret of good quarter-mastering. Explain how this is achieved in your own Troop or Group.

B 1. Have assisted the Camp Quartermaster at a Troop Camp or Pack Holiday of at least five days duration.

2. Understand and be prepared to demonstrate the care of all equipment in camp:
   (a) Ropes, for example coiling and hanking, inspection and storing.
   (b) Tentage, for example emergency guyline repairing, emergency tear repairing and inspection.
   (c) Tools, for example sharpening and cleaning, inspection and storing.
   (d) Cooking equipment, for example cleaning, inspection and storing.

continued overleaf . . .

3. Understand and demonstrate how to keep simple efficient records in camp including issue and return of all equipment.
4. Understand and be prepared to demonstrate how to care for all other special equipment in camp, for example uniforms, hiking kit, climbing kit and canoes.
5. Produce a set of menus covering 48 hours in camp. Be prepared to discuss them with the examiner.
6. Describe how you would deal with storage of food in camp.
7. Submit to the examiner a list of tools you would take to camp to effect emergency repairs of all equipment. Justify your inclusion of each item in the list.
8. Understand that general tidiness is the secret of good quarter-mastering. Explain how this was achieved in the camp at which you helped the Quartermaster.

Radio Technician

Pursuit

To gain the badge you must complete all the requirements in one of the following alternatives:

A

1. Construct a radio receiver with at least two stages. A soldering iron should be used in the construction.
2. Measure the various values of voltage, current and resistance flowing in a simple circuit. Discuss the relationship between voltage, current and resistance.
3. Understand the concept of propagation: typical distances covered on various Amateur bands and their relationship to time of day or night.
4. Demonstrate a knowledge of the various types of Amateur Radio antennas and construct a simple dipole antenna.
5. (a) Know the conditions regulating the issue of Amateur Radio Licences.

   (b) Demonstrate an understanding of good operating techniques.

   (c) Discuss with the examiner the causes of radio and television interference and the steps that might be taken to minimise these effects.

   (d) Show that you know what safety precautions should be taken whilst working with electrical equipment.

B

Pass the Radio Amateurs Examination.

Rock Climber

Pursuit

1. Show your knowledge of ropes used in rock climbing including:

(a) British Standard and UIAA specifications and breaking strains and lengths;

(b) the care of climbing rope, including coiling, storage and recognition of a damaged section and when a rope should be discarded.

2. Demonstrate your ability to tie yourself to:
   (a) a climbing harness or climbing belt;
   (b) a rope directly using a figure of eight knot.
3. Demonstrate your ability to select, test and make the following:
   (a) spike belay, using main ropes;
   (b) thread belay using a suitable sling and karabiner;
   (c) a running belay using chocks, nuts or similar devices;
4. Show your understanding of the calls used in rock climbing.
5. Demonstrate your ability to abseil down a rock face (not less than 10 metres) with a safety rope.
6. Take part in at least five rock climbs of a standard not less than difficult, such climbs must be led by an experienced climber who will judge and report on your competence.
7. Be fully conversant with the contents of the publication *Safety on Mountains* (British Mountaineering Council).
8. Understand different rock types and the effects of weather.
9. Be able to discuss the various pressures of cliff environments, how the action of users affects the environment and what measures can be taken by a climber to reduce conflicts and promote conservation.

Seamanship

JUNIOR SEAMAN
Interest
(Green background)

1. Swim 50 metres and stay afloat for five minutes.
2. Explain the safety rules that apply to boating and the effects of winds, tides and current.
3. Explain the difference between a buoyancy aid and a lifejacket. Adjust to fit and wear one to enter the water from a height of one metre.
4. Complete one of the following:
   (a) Row a dinghy single handed and carry out basic manoeuvres.
   (b) Scull a dinghy over the stern and carry out basic manoeuvres.
   (c) Sail a figure of eight course.
   (d) Qualify for the BCU One Star test.
   (e) Gain the RYA National Dinghy Certificate Scheme Level 1.
5. Carry out an activity using a knot, a bend, a hitch, and a lashing and demonstrate rope sealing.
6. From the list of training activities, complete four items from at least four different sections.

SEAMAN
Interest
(Red background)

1. Hold the Junior Seaman badge or be at least 11½ years of age, and complete requirements 1, 2, 3 and 5 of the Junior Seaman badge.
2. Have some knowledge of rescue by boat or canoe and be able to carry out a simple rescue exercise.
3. Heave a lifeline from a boat, to land within reach of a target six metres away, within two attempts.
4. Know the steering and sailing rules and apply these to the craft being used.
5. Plan and take part in a half-day's expedition or exercise afloat.
6. Complete from the list of training activities:
   (a) One item from the 'Practical skills' section.
   (b) One item from the 'Safety' section.
   (c) Two items from the 'Rule of the road and communications' section.
   (d) A further five items from the remaining five sections.

continued overleaf . . .

LEADING SEAMAN

Pursuit

(Grey background)

1. Hold the Seaman badge or be at least 13 years of age, and complete requirements 1 to 5 of the Seaman badge.
2. Have a knowledge of pilotage, navigation lights, sound signals, tides, currents and eddies appropriate to your local waters and activities.
3. Take care of and maintain a boat or canoe for a period of at least three months.
4. Know how to obtain local weather forecasts, understand their importance and be able to recognise signs of changing weather.
5. Take charge of a party participating in an activity afloat.
6. Complete from the list of training activities:
   (a) One further item from the 'Practical skills' section.
   (b) Two further items from the 'Safety' section.
   (c) One further item from the 'Rule of the road and communications' section.
   (d) A further four items from the remaining five sections.

MASTER SEAMAN

Pursuit

(Gold background)

1. Hold the Leading Seaman badge or be at least 14 years of age, and complete requirements 1 to 5 of the Leading Seaman badge, and undertake one item from the 'Practical skills' section of the training activities.
2. Pass a message to another boat or ashore by visual or radio signal, using the correct procedures.
3. Have a good working knowledge of charts including projection, datum and symbols used.
4. Know the activity rules for expeditions as laid down in *Policy, Organisation and Rules.*
5. Take charge of a two day (one night) expedition on the water, with at least three friends, of which at least 12 hours is to be spent under way.
6. Complete from the list of training activities:
   (a) One further item from the 'Practical skills' section, which must ensure that at least two different water disciplines have been covered in the Seamanship badge scheme.
   (b) Six further items from the remaining seven sections.

PRACTICAL SKILLS

1. Gain The Scout Association B1 Pulling Certificate.
2. Gain The Scout Association B2 Pulling Certificate.
3. Gain The Scout Association B3 Pulling Certificate.
4. Gain The Scout Association B1 Power Certificate.
5. Gain The Scout Association B2 Power Certificate.
6. Gain the RYA National Powerboat Level 2 Certificate.
7. Gain the BCU 2-Star Test (Kayak or Canadian).
8. Gain the BCU 3-Star Test (Kayak or Canadian).
9. Gain the BCU Safety Test.
10. Gain either the BCU Inland or Sea Proficiency Award.
11. Gain the RYA National Dinghy Certificate Scheme Level 2.
12. Gain the RYA National Dinghy Certificate Scheme Level 3.
13. Gain the RYA National Dinghy Certificate Scheme Level 4.
14. Gain the RYA National Dinghy Certificate Scheme Level 5.
15. Gain the RYA National Dinghy or Keel Boat Certificate 2.
16. Gain the RYA National Dinghy or Keel Boat Certificate Level 3.
17. Gain the RYA National Dinghy or Keel Boat Certificate Level 4.
18. Gain the RYA Competent Crew Certificate (practical).
19. Gain the RYA Day Skipper/Watch Leader Certificate (practical).
20. Gain the RYA Motor Cruising Certificate.
21. Gain the RYA National Windsurfing Scheme Level 1.
22. Gain the RYA National Windsurfing Scheme Level 2 (inland or open sea).
23. Gain the RYA Young Sailor Scheme Start Sailing 1 Award.
24. Gain the RYA Young Sailor Scheme Start Sailing 2 Award.
25. Gain the RYA Young Sailor Scheme Start Sailing 3 Award.
26. Gain the RYA Young Sailor Scheme Red Badge.
27. Gain the RYA Young Sailor Scheme White Badge.
28. Gain the RYA Young Sailor Scheme Blue Badge.

Note:

BCU stands for British Canoe Union.

RYA stands for Royal Yachting Association.

SAFETY

29. Demonstrate the H.E.L.P. posture for survival in water.
30. With other members of the Patrol, demonstrate the HUDDLE position for survival in water.
31. Explain how a life jacket works and be able to demonstrate its use.
32. Explain the effects of temperature, wind and water on the human body in cases of hypothermia and exhaustion. List the first aid procedures in these cases.
33. In conjunction with another canoeist, demonstrate two methods of canoe rescue.
34. Heave a lifeline from a boat, to land within reach of a target eight metres away, twice within three attempts.
35. Acting as an assistant in a rescue exercise, board a stranded craft and bring it ashore single-handed.

continued overleaf . . .

36. Under sail, demonstrate 'man overboard' drill using a suitable object.
37. Using a training manikin demonstrate the correct method of ventilation.
38. Demonstrate capsize drill in a sailing dinghy.
39. Any other one activity of a similar nature and level of achievement as agreed by the Patrol Leaders' Council.
40. Understand and explain how you effect a rescue using the following methods: reach, throw, wade and row.
41. Explain the dangers associated with polluted water (such as Weil's disease, blue-green algae).

BOATS AND CONSTRUCTION

42. Name the parts of a boat and its equipment, prepare it for a water activity and use it.
43. With other members of your Patrol clean and paint a boat.
44. Under supervision carry out repairs to a boat.
45. Demonstrate an ability to do simple sail repairs, using a palm and needle.
46. Rig a sailing boat and name the parts of the gear.
47. Build and maintain a canoe or boat.
48. Under supervision carry out routine maintenance on an outboard motor and demonstrate the proper fitting to the transom of a boat.
49. Whilst afloat, construct and hoist a jury rig from available materials in the boat. Sail the jury rigged boat 500 metres.
50. Make a boat's bag or sail bag.
51. Build and demonstrate a working model of a boat.
52. Any other one activity of a similar nature and level of achievement as agreed by the Patrol Leaders' Council.

NAVIGATION

53. Read a mariner's compass and have a knowledge of variation and deviation.
54. Demonstrate how a position may be found by two bearings.
55. Demonstrate use of tide tables and tidal stream atlases.
56. Explain the system of strip maps of canals and rivers. Use one of these charts to plan an expedition.
57. Demonstrate how compass error can be found from a transit bearing.
58. Plot your position using a Decca or satellite navigation system.
59. Plot your position at sea. Understand the 'cocked hat' principle.
60. Use a sextant to measure vertical angles.
61. Complete a navigation exercise by day on water and know how to find north by sun or stars.
62. Demonstrate how to take soundings in local waters, both with leadline and pole.
63. Any other one activity of a similar nature and level of achievement as agreed by the Patrol Leaders' Council.

ROPEWORK AND TRADITION

64. Hoist the colours for a Sea Scout Group. Pipe the 'Still' and 'Carry On' on a Bosun's Call.
65. Demonstrate three further calls commonly used in a Sea Scout Group.
66. Make a Sailmaker's whipping and one other type of whipping.
67. Make an eye splice and a back splice.
68. Make a short splice.
69. Demonstrate, in a nautical setting, the following and their correct uses: clove hitch, rolling hitch, fisherman's bend and a form of stopper knot.
70. Make a rope fender or a decorative piece of ropework, for example a lanyard.
71. Demonstrate the correct method of maintaining and stowing ropes. Explain the differences in usage and stowage of natural and synthetic ropes.
72. Any other one activity of a simlar nature and level of achievement as agreed by the Patrol Leaders' Council.

METEOROLOGY

73. Know the Beaufort wind and sea scales.
74. Identify the basic types of clouds. Explain how they are formed, how wind speed is measured and how weather can affect water activities.
75. Identify the weather associated with frontal systems in the United Kingdom, and be able to explain the meaning of the terms used in describing a weather map (col, ridge, trough, occlusion and so on).
76. Explain how temperature and pressure are measured. List the units used for each, and demonstrate conversion between centigrade and fahrenheit.
77. Identify the weather conditions associated with the movement of air masses over the United Kingdom (polar/tropical, maritime/ continental).
78. Derive the geostrophic wind speed from information given on a synoptic chart and discuss its relationship to wind on land and in coastal waters.
79. Be able to interpret a weather map and identify at least two natural signs for weather changes in your area. Set up a simple weather station and keep a log book of your recordings over a period of a month.
80. Record a shipping forecast, make a weather map from it, and be able to interpret it.
81. Any other one activity of a similar nature and level of achievement as agreed by the Patrol Leaders' Council.

EXPEDITIONS

82. Demonstrate a knowledge of the pulling orders used in single banked boats and take charge of a pulling boat.
83. Be able to steer and manoeuvre a boat, canoe or dinghy.
84. Complete a one-day expedition by canoe, pulling boat or sailing dinghy with friends.
85. Form part of a crew of a pulling boat for an expedition of not less than 24 hours duration, to include a night spent in camp.
86. Form part of a crew of an offshore cruising vessel for a trip of not less than 24 hours duration, to include at least one night afloat.

continued overleaf . . .

87. Take charge of a boat with crew and, in response to a distress call, take the boat away, steer a short compass course and pick up a small object from the water.
88. Any other one activity of a similar nature and level of achievement as agreed by the Patrol Leaders' Council.
89. Form part of a crew on an inland cruising vessel for a trip of not less than 48 hours duration to include two nights afloat.

RULE OF THE ROAD AND COMMUNICATIONS

90. Know the rules for getting afloat on tidal waters and those of access to inland waters.
91. Know the distress, storm, fog and danger signals.
92. Know the International Buoyage System (IALA).
93. Know the sound signals used by powered vessels, underway or at anchor.
94. Know the navigation lights carried by different types of vessels. Identify at least three different types from the lights displayed.
95. Have a working knowledge of the International Yacht Racing Rules, and the Portsmouth Yardstick Handicapping System.
96. Know the effects of currents on non-tidal waterways and the effect of heavy rain upriver, danger levels, rapids and wild water on two rivers.
97. Be able to advise on suitable moorings and anchorages locally for different types of craft and emergency landing places for small craft.
98. Explain the system of sea lanes in National and International waters.
99. Obtain a Radio Yacht Licence.
100. Any other one activity of a similar nature and level of achievement as agreed by the Patrol Leaders' Council.

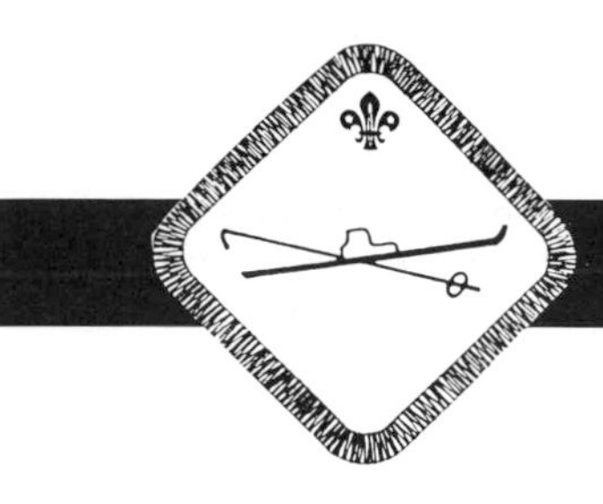

Skier

Interest

A Downhill

1. Demonstrate the following:
   - (a) How to carry skis correctly;
   - (b) Climbing (by side-stepping or herring-bone);
   - (c) Turning around ('star' or 'kick' turn);
   - (d) Straight schuss descent;
   - (e) Snowplough glide descent to a controlled stop;
   - (f) Non-stop, no falls descent with four linked consecutive, right and left, snowplough turns;
   - (g) Correct use of a tow ('button' and/or 'T' bar).
2. Have an understanding of the 'Skier's Code'.
3. Know the procedure to follow in case of an accident.
4. Know how ski bindings work and where to check for correct adjustments.
5. Know how to fit and adjust ski boots correctly.
6. Describe the appropriate clothing for different skiing conditions and surfaces.
7. Understand the importance of staying together when in a group and be fully aware of the dangers of a mountain environment.

Notes:

(i) Skiing may be done on snow or artificial slopes.

(ii) All skiing should be done on runs that are either GREEN or BLUE standard.

(iii) Advice on European and other equivalent awards is available from the Activities Office at Gilwell Park.

B Cross-country

1. Demonstrate the following:
   - (a) How to carry skis correctly;
   - (b) Climbing by side-stepping and herring-bone techniques;
   - (c) Turning around using a star turn;
   - (d) A straight schuss descent;
   - (e) A shallow angle ascent and traverse;
   - (f) Basic diagonal stride;
   - (g) Snowplough glide descent to a controlled stop;
   - (h) Demonstrate an ability to move freely by completing a conducted tour of a 5km forest circuit.
2. Have an understanding of the 'Skier's Code' booklet and the following 'Rules of the Track'.
   - (a) Ski on the right, overtake on the left.
   - (b) Always step out of the tracks when you stop.
   - (c) Where indicated, always follow the direction of the arrows.
   - (d) The downhill skier has the right of way.

continued overleaf . . .

(e) Keep in the tracks and do not destroy the central reservation.

(f) Keep your poles close to your body when passing or overtaking another skier.

(g) On downhill runs, keep within your ability, pay attention to the terrain and visibility and respect other skiers.

3. Know the procedure to follow in the case of an accident especially when away from immediate help, for example, in a forest.
4. Know how cross-country ski bindings work and how to check for correct adjustments.
5. Know how to fit and adjust cross-country ski boots.
6. Describe the appropriate clothing for different weather conditions and skiing surfaces.
7. Be aware of the dangers of the forest environment in winter and understand the importance of skiing in a group and of never skiing a cross-country circuit alone.

Notes:

(i) Skiing may be done on snow or artificial surfaces.

(ii) All skiing should be done in low level terrain such as fields, roads, tracks, forest and so on.

(iii) Possession of the Bronze (1 Star) Cross-country Ski Test of the British Ski Federation (or equivalent) qualifies for this badge.

Advanced Skier

Pursuit

A Downhill

1. Hold the Skier Badge (Downhill option).
2. Demonstrate the following:

(a) Diagonal traverse to left and right;

(b) Direct controlled sideslip for at least 5 metres (leading with both left and right boot);

(c) Diagonal controlled sideslip for at least 5 metres (leading with both left and right boot);

(d) Six consecutive basic swing or parallel turns;

(e) Non-stop, no falls descent through six open gates;

(f) Swing to the slope stop from a steep traverse to both left and right;

(g) Skiing rough terrain including bumps (for example, a mogul field).

3. Explain how ski and boot bindings work and demonstrate their correct adjustment.
4. Understand ski construction and be able to demonstrate the following simple maintenance:

(a) Repairs to the base;

(b) Sharpening the edges;

(c) Waxing.

5. Understand and explain the need for proper party control.
6. Understand the dangers of the mountain environment and be able to explain the folowing terms and, where appropriate, know their prevention and treatment:
   (a) Hypothermia;
   (b) Frostbite;
   (c) Wind chill;
   (d) Lapse rate.
7. Be aware of the problems of less able skiers and of your responsibilities to them and understand the dangers of skiing 'off-piste'.
8. Show a knowledge of, and demonstrate the use of, a ski resort piste map.

Notes:

(i) Skiing should be done on snow wherever possible.

(ii) All skiing should be done on runs that are either BLUE or RED standard.

(iii) Advice on European and other equivalent awards is available from the Activities Office at Gilwell Park.

B Cross Country

1. Hold the Skier Badge (Cross-country option).
2. Demonstrate the following:
   (a) Double poling technique;
   (b) Diagonal ascending traverse to the left and the right;
   (c) Diagonal descending traverse to the left and the right;
   (d) Controlled sideslip for 5 metres leading with either foot;
   (e) Turning around using a kick turn;
   (f) Six linked consecutive snowplough, stem or Telemark turns;
   (g) An ability to move freely over mixed terrain by completing a 10km conducted tour both on and off tracks where possible.
3. Explain how cross country ski bindings and boot bindings work and demonstrate their correct adjustment.
4. Understand cross-country ski construction and demonstrate how to repair the base and sharpen the edges.
5. Describe basic waxing.
6. Understand the need for proper party control and explain your responsibilities when there are less able skiers in your party.
7. Understand the dangers of the forest and mountain environment and be able to explain the following terms and, where appropriate, know their prevention and treatment:
   (a) Hypothermia;
   (b) Frostbite;
   (c) Wind chill;
   (d) Lapse rate.
8. Show a knowledge of, and demonstrate the use of, a map and compass.

Notes:

(i) All skiing should be done on snow.

(ii) All skiing should be done in upland terrain.

(iii) Possession of the Silver (2 Star) Cross-country Ski Test of the British Ski Federation (or equivalent) automatically qualifies for this badge.

(iv) Possession of the Bronze (1 Star) Cross-country Ski Test of the BSF automatically qualifies for parts 2 (a) and 2 (f).

Smallholder

Interest

To gain the badge you must complete all the requirements in one of the following alternatives:

A 1. Have a good knowledge of the farming practices of your locality, with a more detailed knowledge of those of the parish in which you live.

2. Know the farm organisation and daily and seasonal operations of a farm of your own choice, with special reference to the livestock, crops, cultivations and machinery and labour force of the farm.

3. (a) Discuss with the examiner and give an account of the changes in the farm practices that have taken place recently in the parish, with particular reference to the starting or giving up of crops or types of stock, and the reasons for these changes.

   (b) Produce a set of 12 photographs, of at least eight different seasonal jobs that cover a whole year, taken by yourself on the farm of your choice (simple snapshots are sufficient). Give a brief description of what they represent.

B 1. Cultivate out of doors an area of at least 15 square metres for a year, during which time three kinds of hardy annual flower, three kinds of vegetable and two kinds each of bulbs, herbacious plants and flowering shrubs or roses shall be grown successfully. (As an alternative, eight types of vegetable may be grown.)

2. Discuss with the examiner the work you have done in your garden and the results achieved.

Note:The examiner should visit the garden at least four times during the year.

C 1. Keep any kind of livestock for a year.

   (a) If the animal is a small animal (dog, cat, rabbit, mouse and so on) know its breeding habits, and how the animal should be fed, housed exercised and trained.

   (b) If the animal is a farm animal (for example a horse, cow, sheep, pig or goat) know how it should be fed and housed, its breeding habits and economic use. Show you know how to handle the animal (for example ride a horse, milk a cow).

(c) If the animal is a bird:

(i) Cage bird - keep, feed and care for the bird.

(ii) Domestic bird (hen, bantam or pigeon) - keep, feed and care for the bird. Know the uses of the bird and how to handle it.

(d) If the animals are bees, keep and manage a hive of bees for a year. Know their uses and show some of the produce.

(e) If the animals are fish:

(i) Set up and keep an aquarium containing a proper balance of fresh water fish and plant life. (A minimum stock of three fish is to be kept.)

(ii) Discuss with the examiner the keeping of the aquarium during the year, with particular reference to the results obtained.

Notes:

(i) The examiner should be appointed at the start of the twelve-month period.

(ii) Headquarters will provide, on request, requirements for this badge for a Scout whose needs are not dealt with in those above.

Speleologist

Pursuit

1. Hold the Caver badge.
2. Learn how caves are formed and be able to talk about them with the Examiner.
3. Rig and use a ladder pitch under supervision.
4. Undertake as part of a properly led group six different trips in at least two different cave systems, these to be different from or extensions of, those logged for the Caver badge. Three of these trips should include sections involving vertical pitches. The accounts of these trips to be presented in the same log as that used for the Caver badge.
5. Learn the caving and cave conservation codes and be able to discuss with the Examiner measures that can be taken by participants in the activity to reduce conflict and promote conservation.
6. Make a study on an aspect of speleology agreed with the examiner and discuss your findings (for example fauna and flora found in caves, cave photography or bat conservation).

Note:

Caving and pot holing are potentially hazardous pursuits and Scouts should only undertake this badge if they can gain the necessary experience as a member of a properly organised caving group, run by experienced adult cavers, who will directly supervise any vertical pitches.

Sports

Interest

To gain the badge you must complete all the following requirements:

1. Know the rules or laws of two outdoor or indoor games such as rugby, soccer, netball, cricket, tennis, volleyball, table tennis, badminton. Be capable of acting as an official, such as referee, linesman or umpire, in a game organised for young people (school, youth club, Troop or Pack).
2. Take an active part in two active sports and show reasonable proficiency and evidence of a sportsmanlike approach.
3. Be able to discuss with the examiner the advantages which can be gained from participation in sport and show that you have a good knowledge of two games chosen by yourself.
4. Know the names and performances of two international, national or local sports personalities. Be able to discuss these personalities with the examiner and show that you have made a study or have carried out some research concerning them.

Note:

The Association's Headquarters will provide on request, requirements for this badge for a Scout whose needs are not dealt with in those above.

Sports Enthusiast

Interest

1. Know the rules and laws for a sport, explain them to an examiner and be able to answer questions on specific situations.
2. Know the training levels of the sport you study and what is required at each level, if the sport you have chosen has a training scheme.
3. Have a good background knowledge of the teams and sports personalities of your chosen sport.
4. State equipment required for the sport.
5. Be able to list major events for the sport of your choice.
6. Give a description of events that you have attended.

Survival Skills

Collective Achievement

1. Demonstrate a knowledge of the following:
   (a) Exposure and its treatment;
   (b) The first aid treatment for external bleeding and shock, the correct method of applying mouth-to-mouth ventilation and the dangers involved in moving injured people;
   (c) Construction of different kinds of shelter;
   (d) Types of fire and burning qualities of different woods;
   (e) Rescue signals involving whistle, torch, Morse, air rescues and ground signals to aid a search party.
2. With a group of at least three Scouts take part in a survival exercise lasting approximately 36 hours, during which the group will:
   (a) Construct a shelter of natural materials and sleep in it;
   (b) Cook all meals over a wood fire;
   (c) Cook without utensils or aluminium foil with the exception of a knife;
   (d) Make a collection of edible plants and/or fruit;
   (e) Demonstrate a suitable method of filtering water and its purification;
   (f) Demonstrate methods of finding direction by day or night without a compass.

Notes:

(i) Requirement 1 must be completed before requirement 2 is undertaken.

(ii) Suitable country for this would be wooded lowlands. Wild mountainous country is not intended.

(iii) Alternative activities may be undertaken as agreed by the Patrol Leaders' Council after consultation with the badge examiner.

Swimmer

Interest

1. Perform a standing dive or a straddle jump from the side of the pool, into a minimum depth of 1.5 metres.
2. Swim 200 metres using any stroke without interruption.
3. Swim 50 metres in shirt/blouse and shorts.
4. Swim two of the following strokes:
   (a) 50 metres front crawl;
   (b) 50 metres back crawl;
   (c) 50 metres breast stroke;
   (d) 50 metres butterfly stroke.
5. Surface dive in two metres of water and recover, with both hands, an object from the bottom. Return to the side of the pool holding the object with both hands.
6. Enter the water from the side of the pool by sliding in from a sitting position. Use any floating object for support, take up and hold the Heat Escape Lessening Posture for five minutes.
7. Tread water or float unaided for five minutes and climb out of deep water without using steps or any other assistance.

Note:

(i) Every care must be taken to check the depth of water and the safety of the diving area when taking or practicing for this badge.

(ii) Requirement 6 should be undertaken wearing a swimming costume only.

Advanced Swimmer

Pursuit

1. Pass or have passed the Swimmer badge.
2. Demonstrate both of the following:
   (a) A racing dive;
   (b) A correct backstroke start.
3. Swim 100 metres in less than four minutes.
4. Swim 800 metres, of which 400 metres shall be on the back, and 400 metres on the front or side (no time limit).
5. Surface dive into two metres of water both head first and feet first and swim at least 2.5 metres under water on each occasion.
6. Tread water for four minutes.
7. Take part in an organised swimming activity.

Notes:

(i) A Scout who holds the Swimmer badge and who has qualified for the Silver Swimming Challenge Award of the Amateur Swimming Association qualifies automatically for requirements 1-6 of this badge.

(ii) Every care must be taken to check the depth of water and the safety of the diving area when taking or practicing for this badge.

Water Sports

Pursuit

To gain the badge you must complete one of the following alternatives:

A Qualify for the Watermanship Proficiency Award of the Amateur Rowing Association.

B Qualify for the Snorkel Diver Award of the British Sub-Aqua Club.

C Qualify for the Gold Fin of the Single Fin Award of the British Surfing Association.

D Qualify for the Bronze Grade of the British Water Ski Federation.

E Qualify for the Royal Yachting Association National Windsurfing Scheme Level 1.

Note:

Headquarters will provide on request alternative requirements for Water Sports not catered for above.

World Conservation

Collective Achievement

Carry out these activities as a member of a group of Scouts, preferably as a Patrol project. Carry out one activity from each of the following sections:

SKILL

1. (a) Create a scented garden for a blind person.
   (b) Adopt a pond and carry out conservation work and maintenance, obtaining permission and expert advice as necessary.
   (c) Build a hide, use it for observing wildlife (preferably staying overnight) and report your findings.
   (d) Assist with the preservation of a stretch of water, for example stream or canal.
   (e) Survey a derelict site, recording how nature has started to reclaim it. Plan and, where possible, take action to further reclamation.

KNOWLEDGE

2. (a) Explain the dangers to health of cigarette smoking, alcohol or drugs.
   (b) Explain how different types of pollution in soil affect growing plants. Describe the safeguards that need to be taken.
   (c) Explain the pollution caused by motor vehicles. Describe how this affects people, plants and buildings and, where possible, illustrate your findings.
   (d) Explain the causes of water pollution and the action which could be taken to lessen the effects.
   (e) Explain how governments, industries, and other agencies are helping people to become aware of conservation.
   (f) Explain how trees are useful to man.

UNDERSTANDING

3. (a) Prepare a check list of dos and don'ts for campers and hikers, so that natural things are neither destroyed nor harmed. Give a copy of the list to each Member of the Troop.
   (b) Find out all you can about animals, birds, plants or fish which are in danger of extinction in your own country. Find out what can be done to save them and, if possible, help to do so with expert advice.
   (c) Explain why so many animals in the world are threatened by extinction and suggest what your Patrol can do to assist in their survival.

continued overleaf . . .

(d) Make a list of ways in which the Troop camp could contribute to pollution. Suggest ways of preventing this and arrange for them to be discussed by the Patrol Leaders' Council before your next camp.

(e) Plan and carry out a conservation project with Members of a Venture Scout Unit.

TELLING OTHERS

4. (a) Plan a campaign to conserve energy at home or at shool or work or at camp or at Troop meetings. Support your campaign with posters, displays, information for the press and advertising material.

(b) Help to make a nature trail for a Cub Scout Pack.

(c) Help a Cub Scout Pack to build bird tables or nesting boxes.

(d) As part of the plans for an expedition, devise a project to improve the environment. Carry out the project and report on it at a Parents' Open Evening, or similar occasion.

(e) Survey your local area to find examples of how man has damaged nature. Show how this can be avoided. Send the results of your survey to the appropriate authorities.

(f) Survey your local area to find examples of how man has tried to improve his environment. Send a letter of appreciation to the appropriate bodies.

Notes:

(*i*) *Alternative activities may be undertaken as agreed by the Patrol Leaders' Council.*

(*ii*) *An adult with some expertise in conservation may be consulted to help with the selection of projects and preparation of alternatives.*

World Friendship

Interest

1. Have corresponded regularly (such as about once a month) for not less than six months with a Scout of another country either individually or as part of a Patrol or Troop 'link-up'.
2. Carry out a study of a country of your own choice and discuss with the examiner the differences in the way of life between that country and your own.
3. *Either:*

   (a) Keep an album or scrapbook for at least six months giving illustrated information (gained from correspondence under requirement 1) on Scout activities, sports, home life and national affairs of the other Scout's country.

   Or:

   (b) Submit a set of not less than 20 photographs or colour slides taken by yourself illustrating and explaining Scouting, life, people, customs and scenery of another country.
4. Complete any two of the following:

   (a) Camp or hike for at least seven days with a Scout or Scouts of another country (either in your own or their country) and produce a log book covering this event to include your impressions and knowledge gained of the foreign Scouts and their country or countries.

   (b) Entertain in your home, a Scout or Scouts from overseas.

   (c) Tell the examiner ways in which you have welcomed immigrant young people or visitors from another country at school, sport or in your local community and what you have done to make them feel at home there.

   (d) Give separate informative talks to your Troop and to a Cub Scout Pack (each of at least five minutes duration) on the interest and knowledge gained from your international experiences.

   (e) Make a tape recording of camp fire songs from another country or a simple conversation with a Scout in another language, with the meaning of each sentence in English.

   (f) Devise and run a Troop or Patrol activity based on information gained from an overseas Scout with whom you are in touch or from your own knowledge of another country or countries.

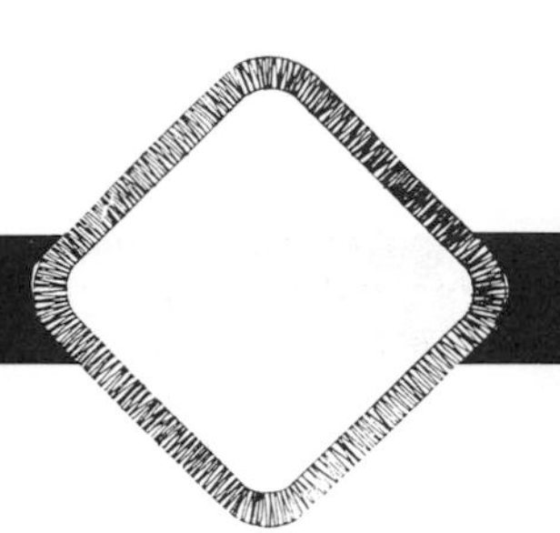

Instructor Badges

Instructor badges are available to all Scouts and in principle are available for all Proficiency badges. The requirements are as follows:

REQUIREMENTS

1. Hold the Proficiency badge in the subject.
2. Have a knowledge of the Proficiency badge requirements sufficient to enable you to instruct a Scout in that subject.
3. Attend a training course covering the technical skills involved and the use of training methods.
4. Assist with the training of Scouts in the subject over a period of at least three months.

Notes:

(i) Requirements 1, 2 and 3 must be completed before a Scout can begin requirement 4.

(ii) For those subjects which do not have a recognised technical skills course, an individual training programme can be arranged with a suitably qualified instructor. The approval of the District Executive Committee is required.

(iii) The gaining of certain external Instructor awards, for example St. John Ambulance, Royal Life Saving Society, National Cycling Proficiency Scheme, and so on, automatically qualifies a Scout for the appropriate Instructor badge.

(iv) A Scout who has already gained one Instructor badge may be exempted from the training methods section of the third requirement.

The badge itself is a green diamond with a yellow border which is sewn behind the Proficiency badge for which the Instructor badge is gained giving it a yellow border.

Instructor badges are gained under arrangements made by an examiner appointed by the District Executive Committee. That may sound very grand and you might wonder why they are not awarded by the Patrol Leaders' Council like most awards. Well, quite simply the skill of instructing, particularly in certain subjects is quite specialised and with over seventy Proficiency badges each Troop would need an awful lot of specialists! Rather than your Patrol Leader or Scout Leader having to search around for the right person the District will do it for you to make life easier. You may gain Instructor badges in two separate subjects if you wish.

Let's have a look at what you have to do:

1. Hold the Proficiency badge in the subject.

Obviously if you want to be able to instruct someone you need to have the skills and knowledge of the subject first. The easiest way to demonstrate you have this is by getting the Proficiency badge, which is why it is the first requirement.

2. Have a knowledge of the Proficiency badge requirements sufficient to enable you to instruct a Scout in that subject.

This requirement is really in two parts, one about knowledge and the second about instructing.

Knowledge - At first the knowledge bit may seem like a repeat of the first requirement, but it may be a long time since you gained the Proficiency badge, so you will need to go back and check that you fully understand each requirement and that your knowledge of the subject is up to date.

Instructing - Instructing is of course the difficult bit and learning the skills of instructing is what this badge is all about. If you have ever tried to teach anyone anything, such as a knot to a younger Scout, you will already know that sometimes it is dead easy but sometimes they just cannot seem to do it. They do it backwards or upside down and both you and they soon get fed up.

This is why you have to learn different methods and techniques of instructing which are particular to your chosen badge. To help you, you will take part in a short special course which will probably be designed specially for you and is part of the next requirement.

3. Attending a training course covering technical skills involved and the use of training methods.

Having to attend a 'training course' may sound like a big task but it probably will not be all that difficult. At the highest level you might choose to attend an Instructor Course run by another organisation such as the St. John Ambulance or British Canoe Union and the advantage of this, even though it may take quite some time and commitment to become an instructor, is that you will then be able to instruct with both organisations and not just the Scouts in the future.

You do not have to do a course with another organisation though and indeed there may not even be one for your subject, so it is fine to do a course locally organised by the District, yourself and your examiner. This 'course' will usually be in three parts, a 'getting started' session, a 'technical skills' session and a 'training methods' session. How much time you spend on each one will depend entirely on the subject you have chosen.

Before you start the course you will already have discussed with your Scout Leader what badge you want to do and arrangements will have been made with the District for an examiner to be appointed. The District may appoint two different people to help you, both an examiner to follow your progress and a coach or instructor who is skilled in your particular interest. When this has been organised for you you are ready to start the course.

GETTING STARTED SESSION

This short session is a chance to meet with the examiner and, possibly, a coach or instructor as well, both to get to know one another and to organise dates, times and the training needed depending on the Proficiency badge you have chosen. Session two, the technical skills session, might also be done at this time.

TECHNICAL SKILLS SESSION

During this session the examiner will want to work with you to see that you have the basic skills of your subject; almost like a revision of the Proficiency badge. So depending on the badge you have chosen this might be an hour on the water to see your canoeing skills or an hour's horse riding if you are an equestrian. The examiner will want you to demonstrate in a practical way you have the technical skills you need. If you are confident this should be really easy and good fun.

TRAINING METHODS SESSION

This session is about training you to instruct others and again what this session consists of will depend entirely on your chosen subject. The session will probably be broken down into two parts, how to help other people learn and skills specific to your subject.

The 'how to help people learn' part will probably cover:

- how people learn by listening, doing and practicing;
- how to break learning down into simple steps;
- why training aids are useful and how to use them;
- why encouragement is important;
- setting reasonable targets;

and many other useful principles for teaching any subject.

The specific skills part could be anything depending on the badge, but if you take the Swimmer badge for example it might include:

- how to get people confident in the water;
- exercise that could be done on the pool side and in the water;
- safety factors;
- simple knowledge of how the body works;
- how much time should be spent on one session.

Although you will need somewhere fairly quiet and equipped with the necessary training materials to go through the first part, the second part is quite likely to be another practical session where you can put what you are learning into practice.

You are now ready for the last part of the badge.

4. Assist with the training of Scouts in the subject over a period of at least three months.

One of the most important things to remember about this part of the award is summed up in the first word 'assist'. It does not say 'be totally responsible for' or 'get everyone through the Proficiency Badge in' and it is important to remember this particularly if you choose an outdoor activity where the responsibility should quite rightly be taken by an adult.

You will, however, be expected to put what you have learnt into practice and show at the end of three months that some of the Scouts you have helped train have gained from your training. It is probably best to keep a simple log of the training you have given in your chosen subject.

Having completed all that the examiner should be happy to award you your Instructor badge.

EXCEPTIONS TO THE RULE

We said at the beginning of this introduction that Instructor badges are available for all Proficiency badges 'in principle'.

Unfortunately for a very few Proficiency badges it may not be possible to get an Instructors badge, for example where age ranges do not permit younger Scouts who you would train to take part in an activity, such as Paragliding. On occasions it might just not be practical, for example you would find it very difficult to be an instructor of the Interpreter badge if the Scouts you were trying to instruct speak a different language!

However, these exceptions are very few and far between and if you would like to have a go at something have a chat with the Scout Leader. The District

Executive Committee, who appoint Instructor badge examiners, and your examiner will do all they can to help you.

NOTES FOR SCOUT LEADERS AND DISTRICT EXECUTIVE COMMITTEES

Take up on Instructor Badges over the last few years has not been particularly high which is a shame as an instructor qualification could stand a Scout in good stead both for future employment and for life.

There are, of course, many possible reasons for this low take up, but the following can be easily identified and perhaps with a little effort could be dealt with.

Having to contact a District Executive Committee is a daunting task for any Scout (and even some Scout Leaders!). At District level this can be helped by:

- making sure the Executive Committee is aware of its responsibility in this field;
- making an individual responsible for a task;
- advertising that responsible member's name and contact telephone number to both Scout Leaders and Patrol Leaders' Councils.

The prospect for Scouts to work, perhaps by themselves, with people they don't know is also daunting. This can be helped by:

- holding information evenings at a District level which all interested Scouts can go to;
- holding joint sessions of the training course, particularly the second session;
- advertising when one or two Scouts are interested to see if others wish to come along;
- selecting examiners the Scouts know, for example the Scout Leader;
- distinguishing between examiners, coaches and instructors;
- wherever possible, selecting coaches and instructors the Scouts know;
- involving other Scouts, not going for the badge itself, as trainees.

Clearly it is also a great advantage if people chosen to be examiners, coaches and instructors are used to working with and, indeed, training young people, and are made fully aware of the level that is likely to be achieved.

In many cases though, if numbers remain low, to give each Scout the opportunity to gain an Instructor badge, without having to wait months for a course or for someone else to show an interest, individual arrangements will need to be made and it is vitally important that parents, Scout Leaders and so on are kept fully informed particularly if a Scout is to undertake something alone. It is strongly recommended in such situations that a separate examiner and coach or instructor are used who will both attend all sessions and that the individual Scout is at least accompanied by one other Scout so that practical experience can be gained with a trainee. It is also important that every effort is made to involve other Scouts in the practical exercises and experiences of the course.

Further information on any aspect of Instructor badges is available from the Programme and Training Department at Gilwell Park.

Proficiency Badge Index

Proficiency Badge Index

INSTRUCTOR BADGES

An Instructor badge is available for each Proficiency badge, although no more than two Instructor badges may be acquired by one person.